HOW TO FORM A LIMITED COMPANY

THIRD EDITION

How to Form a Limited Company

Third Edition

- Example Memorandum of Association
- Example Articles of Association
- Example Registers
- Agenda for First Meeting of Directors

... Everything you need!

Brian O'Kane BComm FCA

Oak Tree Press
Dublin

Oak Tree Press
Merrion Building
Lower Merrion Street
Dublin 2, Ireland
http://www.oaktreepress.com

© 1999 Brian O'Kane
First edition 1993, second edition 1995

This edition ISBN 1-86076-153-4

A catalogue record of this book is available from the British Library.

All rights reserved. No part of this publication may be reproduced or transmitted in any form or by any means, including photocopying and recording, save for the exclusive use of the purchaser in the course of his/her enterprise, without written permission of the publisher. Such written permission must also be obtained before any part of this publication is stored in a retrieval system of any nature. Requests for permission should be directed to Oak Tree Press, Merrion Building, Lower Merrion Street, Dublin 2, Ireland.

The contents of this publication are believed to be correct at the time of printing. No responsibility for loss occasioned to any person acting or refraining from action as a result of the material in this publication can be accepted by the author or publishers.

Printed in the Republic of Ireland by e print Ltd.

Contents

Introduction 1
   What is a Limited Company? 1
   Why Form a Limited Company? 3
   When to Form a Limited Company? 4
   What Does it Cost? 5

Forming your Own Company 6
   Choosing a Company Name 6
   Registering a Business Name 7
   What Will the Company Do? 9
   Drafting an objects clause 9
   The Memorandum of Association 11
   Example Memorandum of Association 14
   The Articles of Association 19
   Example Articles of Association 21
   The Shareholders 23
   Share capital 24
   The Directors 25
   The Secretary 26
   The Companies Capital Duty Statement 27
   The Declaration of Compliance 27
   Submitting the documentation 28
   Checklist for incorporation documentation 29

After Incorporation 30
The Company Seal 30
The Certificate of Incorporation.. 30
The Company's Registered Number............................... 30
Publication in Iris Ofigúil.. 31
The First Directors' Meeting.. 31
Example Agenda for the First Directors' Meeting 33
Example Minutes of the First Directors' Meeting 34

The Statutory Books 35
The Register of Members 36
The Register of Directors.. 37
The Register of Secretaries 38
The Register of Directors' and Secretaries' Interests..... 39
The Register of Debenture Holders 40
Registration of Charges 41
Change of Registered Office 41

Accounting and Tax Requirements 43
The accounts and the audit.. 43
Taxation and the limited company................................... 45

Forming a Company through an Agent................................. 47
A purpose-made company 47
A "ready-made" company.. 48

Appendix 1: Registrar of Companies 50
Summary of Filing Fees.. 50

Appendix 2: Table A — Articles of Association 52

Appendix 3: Table B — Memorandum of Association 89

Introduction

The Oak Tree Press Enterprise series, of which the first book *Starting a Business in Ireland* was published in mid-1993, was born out of the frustration of dealing with the bureaucracy and form-filling that surrounds starting a business today.

Many potential entrepreneurs are put off the idea of self-employment because they do not understand the legal requirements with which they are expected to comply — indeed, in many cases, they have difficulty in even getting information on the requirements. Others fall foul of the rules and find their working days spent fighting red tape over trivia.

Nonetheless, the rules exist. They will not go away. They will not make exceptions for you. So the Enterprise series is intended to provide guidance through the maze.

How to Form a Limited Company has a very specific aim. This updated third edition is designed to take you step-by-step through the formation of a private company limited by shares, to the stage where the company is ready to commence trading.

Most limited companies are formed by accountants, solicitors or professional company registration agents. However, forming your own company is not difficult, provided you follow some simple guidelines. And, by doing it yourself, you can make savings on professional fees with only a modest time investment on your own part. When you are starting out, saving money is always important!

What is a Limited Company?

A limited company is one form of business. Others include:

- Sole trader
- Partnership
- Unlimited company
- Co-operative.

The principal difference between a limited company and the other forms of business lies in the extent of the liability of the members — the people who own the business.

If an individual incurs a debt, he or she is usually liable to repay it in full from his or her personal resources. Similarly, a business that incurs debts is normally liable to repay them in full from its own resources — but the members of the business may also be made liable to repay the business's debts in full from their personal resources.

Legally speaking, the company differs from the sole trader or the partnership in that the company is regarded by the law as a "person" separate and distinct from its members. Of course, that should mean that the members of the company cannot be made liable for company debts at all, since technically they are someone else's debts. But few businesspersons would trade with a company whose members could not be made liable to some extent, so company law has developed a system whereby company members can be made liable for company debts to a limited extent.

Limited liability, a concept developed in the 19th century, restricts the extent to which the members of a business can be made personally liable for the debts of the business. If the business is a company "limited by shares" (the most popular form of limited company), each member holds shares in the company. The maximum to which a shareholder of the company can be made personally liable for company debts is the amount he or she owes the company for any shares he or she has taken or has agreed to take. In this way, the members are protected from losing everything they own in the event of a failure in a company in which they have a share.

However, it is not only the shareholders who need to be protected if business is to be encouraged. Those who deal with the company, particularly those who extend credit to the company, its bankers or trade creditors, for example, need to be assured that the members of the business will not abuse the limited liability they enjoy to the detriment of third parties.

This is achieved in a number of ways, for example:
- By legislation, which imposes increasingly strict responsibilities, duties, and disclosure obligations on directors of limited

companies and heavy penalties for non-compliance or breach of legislation

- By legislation, which requires regular formal disclosure of information relating to the financial performance and condition of the company.

A limited company can be public or private. The formation requirements for public companies differ from those for private companies. Public companies usually begin as private companies, and convert in order to allow their shares to be traded more widely, including on the Stock Exchange. This book deals exclusively with the formation of private companies.

Note that the European Communities (Single-Member Private Limited Companies) Regulations 1994 (SI No. 275 of 1994) came into effect in October 1994, allowing the formation of private limited companies with only one member (as against the previous requirement for two members).

Why Form a Limited Company?

Probably the single most important reason for forming a limited company is to avail of the protection of limited liability. By forming a limited company through which a business will be managed, the shareholders can protect those other assets they own which they have not invested in the company.

The second reason is taxation. The tax treatment of profits earned by limited companies can, in some circumstances, be more favourable than the treatment of similar profits in other forms of business. The 10 per cent rate of Corporation Tax for manufacturing and some service companies and the Business Expansion Scheme are two examples.

Other reasons for forming a limited company are:

- Acceptability — a limited company is the most usual form of business and is considered an acceptable means to manage a business. Other forms of business may not be as acceptable to some of those with whom you may wish to trade
- Prestige — the formation of a limited company by an entrepreneur indicates a commitment to his or her business which is accorded a high degree of prestige in the market-place

- Protection of name — if the name under which you wish to trade gives you a competitive advantage (see *Choosing a company name* on page 6), the best way to protect it is to form a company with that name.

There are disadvantages, too. The principal disadvantages are:

- The need to prepare annual accounts in a prescribed format
- The need to disclose information about the business
- In certain circumstances, the tax treatment of income earned through a company and passed to shareholders or directors as fees or salaries may be less favourable than if the income were earned by the individual directly.

A careful decision as to whether a limited company is appropriate must be made when setting up a business. Advice on that decision will vary depending on the circumstances of each individual case and is beyond the scope of this book.

When to Form a Limited Company?

There is no best time to form a limited company. Many will advise that a business should start out as a limited company, rather than as, say, a partnership and later convert.

However, that decision can only be taken against the background of your own resources and needs. There may be tax advantages in postponing the formation of a limited company, but these may be outweighed by difficulty in obtaining credit as a sole trader or in separating business and personal assets.

When you do decide to form a limited company, remember to allow plenty of time between your decision and the date when you plan to commence trading as a limited company. It takes about four weeks to form a limited company (certain company registration agents and other regular users of the service can form a company in 10 days, by complying with certain requirements). Buying a company "off the shelf" from a registration agent can provide an instant solution, but the advantage of this can soon be lost if you subsequently wish to change the name of the ready-made company, since the company cannot trade under the new name until the consent of the Minister for Enterprise, Trade and

Employment has been obtained, you have paid the appropriate fee and the Registrar of Companies has issued a new Certificate of Incorporation.

What Does it Cost?

At the time of writing, forming a limited company yourself costs £51 — plus your time, of course. The cost is broken down as follows:

	£	€
New Companies Registration Fee	50.00	63.49
Capital Duty (Minimum)*	1.00	1.27
Total	51.00	64.76

* Capital duty is charged at a rate of one per cent of actual value of goods or assets contributed in return for shares in the company, less any liabilities which have been taken over or discharged by the company in consideration of that contribution, subject to a minimum of £1.00 (€1.27).

In addition, there will be other costs relating to typing and copying of documents, postage etc. Since these will vary according to your own situation, they are not included in the £51 above.

Furthermore, the amount of the share capital that you and your fellow shareholders will subscribe to the company is not included above, since it is not a "cost", but an investment.

To buy a limited company "off the shelf" from a registration agent, or to have one formed to your own requirements, will add the cost of the agent's fees. Allow about £200 (€254) to buy a company off the shelf — more if you have specific requirements that mean the company must be formed specially.

As you can see, forming a limited company yourself can save you money — worth thinking about when setting up in business for the first time!

Forming your Own Company

The steps involved are:

- Decide on a name for your company
- Define the purpose for which the company is being formed
- Prepare the Memorandum of Association
- Prepare the Articles of Association
- Submit Form A1 to the Registrar of Companies, together with the Memorandum and Articles of Association and a cheque covered by a bank guarantee or draft, made payable to the Registrar of Companies, for the formation fees.

If your application to form a company is accepted, the Registrar of Companies will issue a Certificate of Incorporation. Only after its issue, and the first meeting of the directors of the company, may the company begin to trade.

Choosing a Company Name

The name of a company is one of its most important assets, even though it does not appear in the balance sheet with the other assets. Choose the name of your company carefully. The right name for your company will be:

- Unique
- Easy to remember, pronounce and spell
- Informative
- Image creating.

What name you choose is up to you:

- Use your own name — for example, Frank Kelly — and form a company called *Frank Kelly Limited*
- If your children appear likely to follow you into the business, consider *Frank Kelly and Sons (or Daughters) Limited*

- Use your company name to tell potential customers what you do. *High Speed Signwriting Limited* or *Pet Food Supplies Limited* are more informative than *Frank Kelly Limited*
- Indicate the geographical spread of your work in your company name. *West Cork Forest Advisory Services Limited* combines geographical information with the nature of the business
- Or create an image for your business by using a name that is quirky or intriguing. How many people would have chosen *Apple* as a name for a computer manufacturer?

A Directory of Irish Company Names, which is published by the Registrar of Companies and should be available from your local public library, will tell you which names have already been registered.

You may not use a name which:

- Is identical to the name of an existing company
- Is identical to, or could be confused with, the name of a foreign company which conducts business in Ireland
- Is identical to a well known trade mark
- Could be confused with the name of an existing company, because it is phonetically identical or the difference in spelling is such as to be immaterial
- In the opinion of the Minister for Enterprise, Trade and Employment, is undesirable (no guidelines are given for this)
- Implies State sponsorship
- Uses certain restricted words, such as "Bank", "Banker", or "Banking" (which may only be used with the permission of the Central Bank), "Society", "Co-op", "Co-operative" or "Insurance" (which may only be used with the permission of the relevant sections in the Department of Enterprise, Trade and Employment).

Registering a Business Name

If you wish to trade under a business name other than the company's registered name, for example as *West Cork Forest Advisory*

Services, even though the company is registered as *Frank Kelly Limited*, you must register the business name. This is a requirement of the Registration of Business Names Act, 1963.

Registration of a business name does not:

- Give protection against duplication of the name
- Imply that the name will prove acceptable subsequently as a company name
- Authorise the use of the name, if its use could be prohibited for other reasons — for example, because the name proposed is the trade mark of another person.

Because of this last point, it is important to check whether someone else might have rights in the proposed name before incurring expenditure on stationery, signs etc. Check:

- *A Directory of Irish Company Names*, which is published by the Registrar of Companies and should be available from your public library
- The *Company Index* (available for inspection at the Companies Office, Monday to Friday, 10.00 to 16.30)
- The *Index of Registered Business Names* (available for inspection at the Companies Office, Monday to Friday, 10.00 to 16.30)
- The *Index of Trade Marks* (available at the Patents Office, 45 Merrion Square, Dublin 2 Tel: 01 661 4144).

To register a business name, you must:

- Complete Form RBN1B
- Send it with the prescribed fee, currently £25.00 (€31.74) to The Registrar of Companies.

You can do this when you are sending in the documentation for the formation of the company.

On registration of your business name, you will be issued with a Certificate of Business Name. This must be displayed prominently at the company's registered or principal office and in every branch or premises.

What Will the Company Do?

There is probably little point in forming a company without some purpose in mind, whether it is to be a retailing business, a publishing house, or an oil exploration company. The formal description of the purposes for which the company is formed is the company's "objects".

The objects are to be found in the "objects clause" in the company's Memorandum of Association (which is, broadly speaking, the constitution of the company). The clause lists the purposes, or objects, for which the company was formed, and it is from these objects that the company derives its power to conduct business. If the company conducts any business that is not contemplated in its objects clause, then it is said to be acting *ultra vires*, or beyond its powers.

The consequence of a company conducting business that is *ultra vires* is that not only can the transaction in question be deemed legally void and unenforceable, but also the directors or officers of the company responsible for the *ultra vires* acts can be held personally liable. In other words, they will be personally liable for all *ultra vires* debts, or debts connected with *ultra vires* transactions.

Furthermore, although it is possible to alter the objects of the company, this alteration will not make good any previous *ultra vires* transactions.

Thus, you can readily appreciate the importance of carefully drafting the objects clause. The rigours of the *ultra vires* doctrine can be avoided by the careful use of certain drafting techniques. Avoid future complications by drafting your objects clause properly.

Drafting an objects clause

Drafting a reliable objects clause is not particularly difficult, provided you follow a number of important steps.

First, most companies include a wide number of objects in their objects clauses, even when tied to a specific industry, thus reducing the chances of the activity concerned being outside the objects clause. This can be achieved as follows:

- Set down the primary activities that the company will be involved in. For example, a company might be involved in retailing or publishing or oil exploration
- Extend the primary activities to include peripheral fields of activity. For example, the retailer might include wholesaling and acting as distributors or manufacturers' agents. The publishing company might include newspaper, magazine and book publishing among its activities, as well as perhaps printing, photography, typesetting and bookbinding. The oil exploration company would be well advised to broaden its scope to include all natural resources within its activities, as well as adding processing and distribution to its exploration work
- Redraft to allow for advances in technology. Ten years ago, publishing meant printed material only; now, through advances in technology, computer diskettes and CD-ROMs are becoming acceptable alternative communication media.

Traditionally, the first sub-clause of the objects clause contains the "primary object", that is the main business of the company. Company law may regard objects contained in other sub-clauses as subsidiary to the primary objects clause. Subsidiary objects may only be pursued to promote the primary object of the company.

Second, set out the subsidiary objects or "powers" in the subsequent sub-clauses. For example, the power to borrow money or the power to give guarantees would appear as subsidiary objects or powers. Adapt the subsidiary objects clauses shown in Table B on page 88, or in the example Memorandum of Association that appears on page 14, to your own circumstances and needs.

Third, you can further widen the scope of activities contemplated in the objects clause by including the following sub-clause:

> *To carry on any other trade or business whatsoever which can, in the opinion of the board of directors, be advantageously carried on by the company in connection with or ancillary to any of the businesses specified in the objects clause or the general business of the company.*

This enables the company to carry on any activity, without fear of *ultra vires,* once the board of directors is of the opinion that the activity is for the benefit of the company.

Fourth, it is normal practice to close the objects clause with:

> *Each sub-clause of this clause shall be construed independently of the other sub-clauses hereof and none of the objects mentioned in any sub-clause shall be deemed to be subsidiary to the objects in any other sub-clause.*

This is traditionally included to avoid the possibility that one object might be regarded as primary and all the others as subsidiary. Under this wording, all objects are equal.

Last, it is usual to close an objects clause with a "catch-all" clause, such as:

> *To undertake, provide and carry out any service or contract deemed necessary or advantageous in promoting the objects of the company.*

or:

> *To do all such things as are incidental or conducive to the above objects or any of them.*

Technically speaking, such words are superfluous, since company law will always imply incidental powers, but it is probably wiser to include them in any case.

The Memorandum of Association

The Memorandum of Association, together with the Articles of Association, forms the constitution of a company.

The Memorandum consists of five sections:

- A clause giving the name of the company, with "Limited" or "Teoranta" as the last word of the name
- The objects clause
- A clause stating that the liability of the members of the company is limited
- A clause setting out the amount and division of the company's share capital

- The names and addresses and descriptions of the subscribers — the first shareholders — and the number of shares each has agreed to take (each must take at least one share).

The Memorandum must be signed by each subscriber, of which there must be at least one, in the presence of at least one witness who must also sign. Each subscriber must write opposite his or her name the number of shares he or she has agreed to take. The amount should be written in words (although, in the specimen Memorandum of Association contained in the Companies Acts, the numbers appear as figures).

Note that a company that is formed as a single-member company (that is, with only one subscriber) may convert to the more usual multi-member form by notifying the Registrar of Companies within 28 days of the change. Similarly, a multi-member company may change to single-member status by notifying the Registrar of Companies within 28 days of the change.

The following details are important:

- A margin of 1.5 inches must be left on the left hand side of the text to allow for binding into the company's file at the Companies Office
- The Memorandum must be printed in clear black print on durable paper (use a typewriter with a carbon ribbon or a word processor with a laser printer)
- The Memorandum should be headed as follows:

Companies Acts, 1963 to 1990
Company Limited by Shares
Memorandum of Association of (Company Name)

- The full name of the company must be used. The abbreviations "Ltd." or "Teo." are not acceptable
- The paragraphs of the Memorandum must be numbered consecutively
- The subscriber(s) must give their full names — initials will not do
- The subscriber(s) must sign in their own hand

- The subscriber(s) must write the number of shares they have agreed to take, using the word "one" rather than the numeral "1".

Table B of the First Schedule to the Companies Act, 1963, setting out the form of the Memorandum of Association of a limited company, is reproduced on page 88.

An example of a Memorandum appears below. Clause 2A describes the primary object of this company, which is a publishing company.

Example Memorandum of Association

Companies Acts, 1963 to 1986
Company Limited by Shares
Memorandum of Association of (Company name)

1. *The name of the company is (Company name) Limited.*

2. *The objects for which the company is established are:*
A *(i) To carry on business as printers, publishers, distributors of all kinds of post cards, greeting cards, advertising materials and samples, catalogues, periodicals, newspapers, leaflets, posters and calendars, magazines, sample booklets, books, reports and literature of all kinds; as graphic designers, typesetters, die-sinkers and engravers, as metal type, plate and block makers, as consultants and contractors in all branches of electronic composition, storage, retrieval and transmission of information, as compilers of mailing lists, commercial information and statistics, and as addressing and mailing contractors and circular distributors; as marketing, advertising and publicity agents and contractors, bill posters and hoarding agents, signwriters, illustrators, photographers, lithographers, commercial artists, designers and draughtsmen; as bookbinders, translators, literary, music and drama critics; news-reporters, journalists, press-agents and as newsagents and general stationers; to carry on business as manufacturers or dealers in paper, board, card and plastic products, packaging and promotional materials and computers.*

    (ii) To carry out all aspects of photographic, film and video work including photographic colour printing and the development of any photographic related products.

    (iii) To undertake, provide and carry out any service or contract of works deemed necessary or advantageous in promoting the objects of the company.

    (iv) To acquire and carry on any other business that may seem to the company capable of being conveniently carried on in connection with the above, or which seem calculated directly or indirectly to enhance the value or render more profitable any of the company's property or rights.

B   To purchase, take on lease or in exchange, hire or by any other means, acquire and protect, any freehold, leasehold, or other property, for any estate or interest, any lands, buildings, roads, railways, bridges, waterways, aircraft, vessels, vehicles, machinery, engines, plant, live and dead stock, easements, rights, patents, patent rights, trade marks, brevet d'invention, registered designs, protections or concessions, licences, stock in trade and any real or personal property or rights whatsoever which may be considered necessary, advantageous or useful to the Company.

C   To construct, build, erect, alter, enlarge, demolish, lay down, maintain, any buildings, roads, railways, bridges, walls, fences, banks, reservoirs, waterways and waterworks and to carry out preliminary and associated works or contract, subcontract, and join with others to carry out or complete any of the aforesaid and to work, manage and control the same or join with any person, firm or company in doing so.

D   To borrow, raise or secure the payment of money in such manner as the company shall think fit and in particular to issue debentures, debenture stock, bonds, obligations and securities of all kinds and to charge and secure the same by Trust Deed or otherwise on the undertaking of the Company or upon any specific property or rights, present and future, of the Company including its uncalled capital or by any other means howsoever.

E   To guarantee, support or secure whether by mortgaging or charging all or any part of the undertaking, property and assets both present and future and uncalled capital of the Company or both the performance and discharge of any contract, obligation or liability of a company or of any person or corporation with whom or which the Company has dealings or having a business or undertaking in which the Company is concerned or interested whether directly or indirectly and in particular to give security for debts, obligations or liabilities of any company which is for the time being the Holding Company or a subsidiary of the company or a subsidiary of the Holding Company.

F   To pay and remunerate any person, firm or company for rendering services for and on behalf of this company and to pay costs, charges or expenses incurred or sustained by or in connection with the formation and incorporation of this company and either by cash payments or by allotment to him or them of shares or securities of the company credited as fully paid up or otherwise.

G To invest and deal with the moneys of the company not immediately required for the purpose of its business in or upon such investments or securities and in such manner as may from time to time be determined.

H To draw, make, accept, endorse, discount, negotiate and issue promissory notes, bills of exchange, warrants, bills of lading and other negotiable or transferable instruments.

I To develop, improve, manage, cultivate, exchange, let on lease or otherwise, mortgage, charge, sell, dispose of, turn to account, grant rights and privileges in respect of, or otherwise deal with all or any part of the property and rights of the Company.

J To lend and advance money or give credit to any person, firm or company and on such terms as may seem expedient.

K To enter into and effect any arrangement with any person, firm, company or Government or Government body or authority that may seem conducive to the company's objects and to apply for, promote and obtain from any person, firm, company, Government or Government body or authority any contracts, concessions, privileges, charters, decrees and rights that the company may think is desirable and to carry out and exercise and comply with same.

L To act as agents, brokers and as trustees for any person, firm or company and to establish agencies and branches and appoint agents and others to assist in the conduct or extension of the company's business.

M To provide for the welfare of persons employed or previously employed in or holding office under the company and to grant pensions, allowances, gratuities, bonuses or other payments to officers, ex-officers, employees and ex-employees or the dependants or connections of such persons, to establish and contribute to pensions or benefit funds or schemes for the support of persons aforesaid, to form, subscribe to or support any charitable, benevolent, religious or other establishment calculated to advance the interests of the company or of its officers, ex-officers, employees, ex-employees or dependents or connections.

N To purchase or otherwise acquire and undertake all or part of any of the business, property, goodwill, assets, liabilities and transactions of any person, firm or company carrying on any business that this company is authorised to carry on.

O To undertake and execute the office of nominee, trustee, executor, administrator, registrar, secretary, committee or attorney for any purpose and either solely or jointly with others and generally to undertake, perform and fulfil any office of trust or confidence.

P To accept payment for any property or rights sold or otherwise disposed of or dealt with by the company in whatever form and on such terms as the company may determine.

Q To establish, promote or otherwise assist any company and to promote or otherwise assist any person or firm for the purpose of acquiring all or any of the properties and/or liabilities and for furthering any objects of this company or for the purpose of instigating or opposing any proceedings or applications that may be considered necessary, advantageous or useful to the company.

R To subscribe for, accept, deal in, purchase or sell or otherwise acquire, deal in dispose of or hold shares or other interests in or securities of any company carrying on or proposing to carry on any business within the objects of this company or carrying on any business capable of being carried on so as to benefit this company.

S To enter into any partnership or joint arrangement for sharing profits with any company having objects similar or in part similar to those of this company and to give whatever undertakings are considered necessary by this company.

T To distribute among the members in specie, or otherwise as may be resolved, any assets of the company and in particular, any shares, debentures or securities of other companies belonging to this company or of which this company may have the power of disposing.

U To procure the company to be registered or recognised in any place outside Ireland.

V To do all such things as are incidental or conducive to the above objects or any of them.

W To carry on any other trade or business whatsoever which can, in the opinion of the board of directors, be advantageously carried on by the company in connection with or ancillary to any of the businesses specified in the objects clause or the general business of the company.

The word company, in the clause, except where used in reference to this company, shall be deemed to include any body or persons whether incorporate or not and whether or not domiciled in Ireland or elsewhere.

It is hereby expressly declared that each sub-clause of this clause shall be construed independently of the other sub-clauses hereof and that none of the objects mentioned in any sub-clause shall be deemed to be merely subsidiary to the objects mentioned in any other sub-clause.

Provided always that the provisions of this clause shall be subject to the company obtaining where necessary for the purpose of carrying any of its objects into effect such licence, permit or authority as may be required by law.

3 The liability of the members is limited.

4 The share capital of the company is IR£xxx,000 divided into xxx,000 shares of IR£1.00 each with power to increase or decrease the share capital. The capital may be divided into different classes of shares with any preferential, deferred or special rights or privileges attached thereto, and from time to time the company's regulations may be varied so far as may be necessary to give effect to any such preference, restriction or other term.

We, the several persons whose names, addresses and descriptions are subscribed, wish to be formed into a company in pursuance of this Memorandum of Association, and we agree to take the number of shares in the capital of the company set opposite our respective names.

Names, Addresses and Descriptions of Subscribers	Number of Shares taken by each subscriber
(Name of first subscriber) of (address) ..... in the County of ..... , (business occupation).	One
(Name of second subscriber) of (address) ..... in the County of ..... , (business occupation).	One
Total Shares taken	Two

Signed: (Subscribers' signatures)
Dated the ..... day of ..... , 20..
Witness to the above signatures:

The Articles of Association

Where the Memorandum of Association of a company sets the broad sweep of the company's structure, the Articles of Association spell out the detail. Unlike the Memorandum of Association, it is not a mandatory requirement that companies limited by shares adopt Articles of Association — however, they invariably do.

The Articles of Association set out the regulations for the day-to-day running of the company. Generally, the main contents of the Articles of Association are:

- A reference to "Table A" (see below)
- A statement that the company is a private company
- Share capital — procedures for its allotment and issue, the issue of different classes of share capital with or without different rights
- General meetings of the company — the manner of proposing resolutions and the periods of notice attaching thereto, the manner of voting, where the meetings shall take place
- Borrowing powers — whether any limits, other than those imposed by the company's bankers, apply
- Directors — the manner and period of their appointment, the basis of their remuneration, and their number
- Any indemnities given by the company to directors or officers of the company.

As with the Memorandum of Association, the Articles of Association must be:

- Signed by the subscriber(s), in their own hand, in the presence of at least one witness who must also sign
- Printed (or typed) in clear print on durable paper (allowing a margin of 1.5 inches on the left hand side of the page is advisable)
- Be divided into paragraphs and numbered consecutively
- Be headed:

Companies Acts, 1963 to 1990
Company Limited by Shares
Articles of Association of (Company Name) Limited

The Companies Act, 1963 includes standard form Articles of Association in Table A of Schedule 1 (known simply as "Table A"). Table A is divided into two parts, Part I and Part II. Part I contains the standard form Articles of Association for a Public Company, but is of importance to those forming a Private Company because Part II, which contains standard form Articles of Association for a Private Company, simply adopts parts of Table A Part I without repeating them. Table A, Parts I and II, is reproduced on pages 52-87. It is common to adopt these standard form Articles with little or no modification.

If you decide to adopt Table A, you can either:

- State that Table A will be the Articles of Association of the company, without actually reproducing the text of Table A
- Reproduce the text of Table A as the Articles of Association.

Alternatively, you can start the company's Articles of Association with a clause like this:

> A. *The regulations contained in part I and part II of Table A in the First Schedule to the Companies Acts, 1963 to 1990 (hereinafter referred to as "Table A") shall apply to the Company and together with the regulations hereinafter contained shall constitute the regulations of the Company save in so far as they are varied or excluded thereby.*
>
> B. *Regulations xx and xx (specify the numbers you require) of Table A, part I and regulations xx and xx of Table A, part II shall not apply.*

Then go on to vary those parts of Table A, which while not suitable, you do not wish to exclude altogether.

Alternatively, you can incorporate the exclusions and variations you want in a freshly written Articles of Association, in which case the Articles should start with a clause:

Table A and all its regulations are hereby expressly excluded.

An example of Articles of Association can be found on the page following.

Example Articles of Association

Companies Acts, 1963 to 1990
Company Limited by Shares
Articles of Association of (Company name)

1 A *The regulations contained in parts I and parts II of Table A in the First Schedule to the Companies Acts, 1963 to 1986 (hereinafter referred to as "Table A") shall apply to the Company and together with the regulations hereinafter contained shall constitute the regulations of the company save in so far as they are varied or excluded hereby.*

  B *Regulations 5, 8, 47, 51, 54, 75, 79, 84, 86 and 138 of Table A, part I and regulation 7 in part II of Table A shall not apply.*

2 *The company is a private company.*

3 *The share capital of the company is IR£xxx,000 divided into xxx,000 shares of £1.00 each.*

4 *Any shares may be issued upon the terms that they are or at the option of the company are liable to be redeemed.*

5 *Regulation 53 of Table A, part I, shall apply as if the following words were added at the end thereof "and the fixing of the remuneration of the directors".*

6 *All annual general meetings of the company shall be held in the State.*

7 *A poll may be demanded by the chairman or by any other member present in person or by proxy and regulation 59 of Table A, part I, shall be modified accordingly.*

8 The directors may raise or borrow for the purposes of the company's business such sum or sums of money as they think fit and may secure the repayment of, or raise any such sum or sums as aforesaid by mortgage or charge upon the whole or any part of the property or assets of the company, present and future, including its uncalled or unissued capital, by the issue at such price as they may think fit, of bonds or debentures, either charged upon the whole or any part of the property and assets of the company, or in any other way as the directors may think expedient.

9 The directors of the company shall not be required to retire by rotation and regulations 92 to 100 (inclusive) of Table A, part I, shall be amended accordingly.

10 Unless and until determined otherwise by the company in general meeting, the number of directors of the company shall not be more than seven nor less than two. The first directors will be the persons named in the statement delivered to the Registrar of Companies in accordance with section 3 of the Companies (Amendment) Act, 1982.

11 Where a notice is sent by post, it shall be deemed to have been served at the expiration of forty-eight hours after it was posted and regulation 133 of Table A shall be modified accordingly.

Names, Addresses and Descriptions of Subscribers	Number of Shares taken by each subscriber
(Name of first subscriber) of (address) ..... in the County of ..... , (business occupation).	One
(Name of second subscriber) of (address) ..... in the County of ..... , (business occupation).	One
Total Shares taken	Two

Signed: (Subscribers' signatures)
Dated the ..... day of ..... , 20..
Witness to the above signatures:

The Shareholders

The shareholders are the owners of the company. But that is not to say that they own the company assets, or any part of them. Instead, each shareholder is entitled to a portion, relative to his or her share holding, of the profits of the company whenever a dividend is declared by the directors, as well as a portion of the assets of the company when it is finally wound up.

In small companies, the shareholders are often the directors and manage the business themselves. However, in law, a distinction is drawn between the owners of a business — the shareholders — and the managers — the directors. The latter must account to the former for their actions.

An individual's share holding in a company is evidenced by a share certificate. This is a valuable document since it gives *prima facie* proof of ownership of the shares. The subscriber(s) to the Memorandum and Articles of Association are the first shareholder(s) of the company, and their share certificates are issued at the first meeting of the Board of Directors of the company (see page 31). Generally speaking, shares may not be transferred or sold without surrender of the share certificate.

Most companies, particularly small private companies, have a single class of ordinary share capital with a single vote for each share held. Classes of shares, other than "Ordinary" shares, include:

- Preference shares
- Redeemable shares
- Cumulative Preference shares.

Subject to the company's Articles of Association, which may vary the voting rights between different classes of share, each shareholder has a vote, in proportion to his or her share holding, in the running of the company. This vote may be exercised at the Annual General Meeting or at such Extraordinary General Meetings as may be called.

Unless the shareholder is employed by the company, as a director or executive, he or she has no right to interfere in the day-to-day management of the business except in limited circumstances, such as where there has been a breach of the Articles of Association.

A private limited company is restricted in the number of shareholders it may have. It must have a minimum of one in a single member company, or two otherwise but may not have more than 50, excluding employees and former employees.

Share capital

Authorised capital is the money that the shareholders have invested in the business. It may not be repaid, except in certain specific instances, until the company is wound up.

Every company has an authorised capital. This is the maximum amount that the shareholders can invest. The amount that they actually invest is called the Issued share capital.

Capital duty is payable on the company's issued share capital. Broadly speaking, it is calculated as one per cent of the actual value of the assets contributed in return for shares in the company, less any liabilities that have been taken over or discharged by the company in consideration of that contribution, subject to a minimum of £1.00 (€1.27).

Each shareholder must receive a certificate for his share holding. It is not necessary to issue an individual certificate for each share, but it must be possible from the certificate to identify the shares held.

You can buy share certificate forms in some legal stationers but, for most small companies where there are few shareholders and fewer transactions in the shares, a certificate typed on the company's letterhead will suffice.

Many companies are formed with the absolute minimum issued share capital — a single share for the sole subscriber. Any other capital the company needs to carry on business is then invested by way of loan.

While this may be appropriate in some circumstances, it is better to relate share capital to the long term financing needs of the company, as shown by cash flow projections. More companies get into difficulties because they are inadequately capitalised than for any other reason. Take advice from your accountant on how much capital you need to start your business.

The Directors

The directors of a company are appointed by the shareholders to run the business. There must be at least two directors, even in a single-member company.

In most small companies, the shareholders and directors will be the same people. Indeed, Article 77 of the standard form Articles of Association contained in Table A provides that the company can, in general meeting, set a requirement that all directors will have to hold a certain number of shares in the company. Most companies do set such a qualification. However, if no such share holding qualification is imposed, then it is quite possible, particularly in larger companies, that some directors will have no share holding in the company.

The directors are officers of the company and responsible to the shareholders for the efficient management of the company. They must:

- Carry out their duties at all times with the best interests of the company in mind
- Not make secret profits from their position as directors
- Account regularly to the shareholders for their actions.

The first directors of a company are appointed by the subscribers to the Memorandum and Articles of Association.

Form A1 — the form used to apply for the incorporation of a company — is used to record the appointment of the first directors and the first Secretary.

Note that the consent of the directors, as evidenced by their signatures, is required.

Also required to be disclosed by the directors are:

- Full forename and surname
- Any former forename or surname
- Date of birth
- Business occupation

- Home address
- Details of other directorships, whether the other companies were incorporated in Ireland or elsewhere.

Note also that form A1 requires these details of "Shadow Directors". A shadow director is a person in accordance with whose directions or instructions the directors of a company are accustomed to act (unless they merely do so on advice given in a professional capacity), despite the fact that they are not formally appointed to the board of directors. The scope of this category has not yet been fully determined by company law, but it is clearly possible for a parent company to be found a shadow director of its subsidiary.

Changes in directors, or in their particulars, are notified by:

- Completing Form B10 to show the changes that have taken place
- Sending it with the appropriate fee, currently £10.00 (€12.70), to The Registrar of Companies.

Note that Form B10 is also used to record changes of Secretary to the company.

The Secretary

The Secretary, like the directors, is an officer of the company. He or she is responsible for filing with the Registrar of Companies the various forms and documents needed during a company's life.

Often, the Secretary is also a director of the company, although where a transaction requires the signatures of a director and the Secretary, the same person cannot sign under both positions.

The first Secretary is appointed by the subscribers to the Memorandum and Articles of Association. Form A1 is used to record his or her appointment. Note that the consent of the Secretary, as evidenced by the signature on Form A1, is required. The Secretary must disclose full details of name, previous name, and home address.

Changes of Secretary, or in his particulars, are notified by:

- Completing Form B10, showing the changes which have taken place

- Sending it with the appropriate fee, currently £10.00 (€12.70), to The Registrar of Companies.

The Companies Capital Duty Statement

Form A1 also requires details of:

- Authorised share capital
- Number of shares being allotted
- Nominal (or "face") value of each share class
- Amount of cash or assets received in return for shares issued
- Class of shares
- Consideration for each share.

These details enable the capital duty to be calculated. The Capital Duty Statement should be signed, addressed, and dated by the company secretary or one of the directors.

The Declaration of Compliance

Form A1, which shows the registered office, the names and particulars of the first directors (including shadow directors) and secretary of the company, and contains a Declaration of Compliance, which must be sworn before a Commissioner of Oaths by either:

- A solicitor engaged in the formation of the company, or
- A person named in the form as a director or secretary of the company.

This simply involves the person signing, in the presence of a Commissioner for Oaths, a declaration that all the requirements of the Companies Acts, 1963 to 1990 in respect of the registration of the company have been complied with.

You can find a Commissioner for Oaths by looking in the Golden Pages, or by contacting your solicitor. There is usually a nominal charge for this service.

Submitting the documentation

The final step in the formation of a limited company is the submission of the appropriate documentation to the Registrar of Companies.

You must submit:

- The company's Memorandum of Association (signed by the first shareholder(s) of the company)
- The company's Articles of Association (signed by the first shareholder(s) of the company)
- Form A1, showing the registered office, the names and particulars of the first directors and Secretary of the company and the Capital Duty Statement
- A cheque guaranteed with the Revenue Commissioners, money order or bank draft to cover the fees and stamp duty on the share capital. The cheque or bank draft should be made payable to the Registrar of Companies and crossed. The amount of the cheque will depend, of course, on the amount of capital duty payable, which in turn depends on the amount of money or the value of the assets received in return for shares in the company (see **Appendix 1**).

These all go to the Registrar of Companies. Ideally, you should deliver these yourself, for security. If this is not possible, use registered post.

If all the documentation is in order, your company will be formed and you will receive a Certificate of Incorporation. This will take about four weeks from the time you deliver the documentation to the Companies Office.

If you have made any mistakes in completing Form A1, the Memorandum or Articles, or the Registrar is not clear about what it is you want to do, your documentation will be returned for amendment and re-application. Check back carefully over the steps you have taken and correct where you have gone wrong.

Checklist for incorporation documentation

Double-check that:

- The Memorandum and Articles of Association are clearly printed in black (good quality typing with a carbon ribbon or output from a laser printer will do) on durable paper and that the paragraphs are numbered consecutively
- A margin of about 1.5 inches has been left on each page
- The correct statutes, "**Companies Acts 1963 to 1990**", are quoted at the start of both the Memorandum and Articles of Association
- The full name of the company is given in both the Memorandum and Articles of Association
- The Nominal capital of the company is given in both the Memorandum and Articles of Association
- There is at least one subscriber to the Memorandum
- The Memorandum has been signed by each subscriber
- The Memorandum shows, in writing, the number of shares each subscriber has agreed to take, and their descriptions and addresses
- The Memorandum has been witnessed, signed by the witness, and dated
- The Articles of Association have been signed by all the subscribers, their addresses and descriptions given and their signatures witnessed and dated.
- Form A1 has been completed and signed by the company secretary, the directors (including shadow directors), and the subscribers, either personally or acting through an agent
- The Declaration of Compliance on Form A1 has been properly sworn before a Commissioner for Oaths by either a solicitor involved in the formation of the company or a person named as director or secretary of the company
- The Companies Capital Duty Statement on Form A1 has been completed and signed.

After Incorporation

The Company Seal

Every company must have a Common Seal with its name engraved on it in legible characters. A seal embosses the characters of the company's name on to any document stamped by it. Seals cost approximately £25.00 (€31.74) and are available from a number of manufacturers — check the Golden Pages for details.

The use of the company seal should be restricted to important documents, such as share certificates, trust deeds, contracts, mortgages and the like. When not in use, the seal should be kept in safe custody. It should only be used with the authority of the directors and documents sealed with it should be countersigned by two directors, or a director and the Secretary.

It is not a legal requirement to register the use of the company seal. However, a Register of Use of the Seal, which provides a record of the occasions when the seal was used and the documents it was used to seal, can be useful. The documents sealed should be capable of being identified without doubt from the description contained in the Register. For added security, an identifying number might be written on the document within the area sealed and this number used to index the record of sealing in the Register.

The Certificate of Incorporation

A company does not formally exist until a Certificate of Incorporation has been issued by the Registrar of Companies. This certificate is a valuable document. It should not be defaced or altered in any way. It should be displayed in a prominent position on the company's business premises.

The Company's Registered Number

For official purposes, a company is distinguished not just by its name but also by a number. This is its Registered Number. It appears on the Certificate of Incorporation and is assigned by the Registrar of Companies. A company's Registered Number must be shown on all invoices, correspondence etc.

The company's Registered Number has no connection with the numbers issued by the Revenue Commissioners for VAT, PAYE/PRSI or Corporation Tax.

Publication in Iris Ofigúil

The Registrar of Companies will publish an announcement of the formation of your company in *Iris Ofigúil*, the official bulletin of the State. You will be notified of the publication of this announcement.

This announcement will allow members of the public, to check the company's record at the Companies Office to see who the shareholders and directors of the company are, what the company's objects are, and what other information is recorded.

The First Directors' Meeting

At the first meeting of the Board of Directors:

- The Certificate of Incorporation of the company is produced to the directors
- The Memorandum and Articles of Association are produced to the directors
- The company seal is adopted
- The directors are confirmed in their appointment
- The Secretary is confirmed in his appointment
- Shares are issued to the subscribers
- The auditors are appointed
- A resolution is passed, in the form specified by the bank, authorising a bank chosen by the directors to open and maintain an account on behalf of the company.

If the company has been bought "off the shelf":

- The first directors and Secretary — usually the company registration agent and his staff — resign and new directors and a new Secretary are appointed
- The shareholdings of the subscribers to the Memorandum and Articles of Association — again, usually the company registra-

tion agent and his staff — are transferred to the new owners of the company.

Further items of business may include, where appropriate:

- The production to the directors of a copy of the special resolution changing the name of the company
- The production to the directors of a copy of the amended Certificate of Incorporation, showing the company's new name
- A change of the company's registered office
- A change of the company's accounting date
- The appointment of additional directors.

Example Agenda for the First Directors' Meeting

(Company name)
Agenda for the First Meeting of Directors
to be held at (place)
on (date/time)

1 The company's Certificate of Incorporation to be submitted to the meeting.

2 The company's Memorandum and Articles of Association to be submitted to the meeting.

3 The company seal to be submitted to the meeting and adopted.

4 To confirm (names) as the first directors of the company.

5 To confirm (name) as the first Secretary of the company.

6 To issue share certificates to the subscribers to the Memorandum of Association who subscribed to the shares noted below:
- (First shareholder) xx shares of £x each
- (Second shareholder) xx shares of £x each.

7 To appoint (name) as auditors to the company.

8 To adopt a resolution in the form set out on the attached schedule authorising (name) Bank to open and maintain a bank account in the name of the company.

9 To take any other business.

Example Minutes of the First Directors' Meeting

(Company name)
Minutes of First Meeting of Directors
held at (place)
on (date/time)

Present (names)

1 *The company's Certificate of Incorporation, number xxxxxx, dated xxth day of xxx, 20xx, was submitted to the meeting and noted.*

2 *The company's Memorandum and Articles of Association were submitted to the meeting and noted.*

3 *The company seal was produced to the meeting and adopted.*

4 *The first directors of the company shall be (names).*

5 *The first Secretary of the company shall be (name).*

6 *The subscribers to the Memorandum of Association subscribed to the shares noted below:*
- (First shareholder) xx shares of £x each
- (Second shareholder) xx shares of £x each.

The share certificates noted below were sealed, signed and issued in respect of each shareholder:
- Certificate xx   (First shareholder)
- Certificate xx   (Second shareholder)

7 *(Name) & Co were appointed auditors to the company.*

8 *A resolution in the form set out on the attached schedule authorising (name) Bank to open and maintain a bank account in the name of the company was passed unanimously.*

There being no further business, the meeting adjourned.
    Chairman (signature)   Date xx/xx/20xx

The Statutory Books

A company's Statutory Books are those registers or other books it is required by legislation to keep. They include:

- The Register of Members (also known as the Share Register)
- The Register of Directors
- The Register of Secretaries
- The Register of Directors' and Secretaries' Interests
- The Register of Debenture Holders
- The Minute Book.

In addition, most companies find it useful to keep a number of other registers, which assist the Secretary in his duties, though they are not required by law. These include:

- The Register of Use of Company Seal
- Register of Share Allotments
- Register of Transfer of Shares
- Register of Change of Registered Office.

A secretary is well advised to keep copies of all documents filed with the Registrar of Companies.

For each Register, a bound book is recommended. However, most companies have only a limited number of transactions and to buy a bound book for each register would be wasteful. There are two alternatives:

- To buy a single large bound book and divide it into sections, each section corresponding to a Register
- To buy a loose-leaf binder, using dividers to separate the different sections corresponding to the individual Registers.

If a loose-leaf binder is used, care must be taken to ensure that pages cannot be easily extracted and lost. Pages ought to be pre-numbered to ensure the correct sequence.

The Register of Members

The Register of Members is an important document, providing a formal record of all the shareholders of a company limited by shares.

Legally speaking, a person is not a member of a company until his or her name has been entered on the Register of Members, unless that person is one of the subscribers to the Memorandum of Association, in which case he or she is legally deemed to be a member of the company even if the company fails to place him or her on the Register. Moreover, a member does not cease to be a member until a note of his or her ceasing to be a member is entered in the Register.

Details of the subscribers should be the first entries in your Register of Members. The following particulars must be entered on the Register within 28 days from the date on which the person agreed to become a member, or, in the case of the subscribers, within 28 days from the date of registration of the company:

- The names and addresses of the members
- A statement of the shares held by each member, distinguishing each share by its number, so long as the share has a number, and the amount paid or agreed to be considered as paid on the shares of each member
- The date at which each person was entered on the Register as a member.

The Register must also contain details of:

- The date at which any person ceased to be a member
- If the company has more than one class of shares, the class of shares held by each member.

The Register of Members must be kept at the company's registered office, unless notice of a change in location has been filed with the Registrar of Companies. Form B3 is used to file the change of location and the current filing fee is £10.00 (€12.70).

The Register must be available for inspection by any shareholder of the company for at least two hours daily during business hours, and likewise by any other person on payment of a fee not exceeding 5p (€0.06).

If a shareholder, or any other person, requests a copy of the Register or any part of it, the Secretary must send it to him within 10 days. A fee of no more than 10p (€0.13) per 100 words, or part thereof, may be charged.

A Register of Transfers of Shares is not required by law, but many Secretaries find it useful, particularly where there are large numbers of transfers.

Its purpose is to provide a record of all transfers of shares — that is, sales by one shareholder to another new shareholder — and to act as a check to ensure that all transfers are duly registered, new share certificates issued and the transfer recorded in the company's Annual Return.

A Register of Share Allotments is not required by law, but many company Secretaries find it useful.

Its purpose is to provide a record of all applications for shares in the company, the amounts subscribed for them, and whether or not the applications were successful. The record can then be tied up, both with the company's records of money received and paid out and with the share register itself.

The Register of Directors

The Register of Directors must be kept at the company's registered office. It must be open to inspection by any shareholder without charge for at least two hours daily during business hours, and likewise by any other person, on payment of a fee not exceeding £1.00 (€1.27).

The Register must contain the following information in relation to each director:

- Present surname and forename and any former surnames and forenames
- Date of birth
- Usual residential address
- Nationality
- Business occupation, if any

- Details of any other directorships held, or formerly held, here or abroad, within the preceding ten years.

Former forenames and surnames are names that have been changed by deed-poll, and do not include maiden names of married women, or nicknames.

Changes in the directors or in their particulars must be notified to the Registrar of Companies within 14 days of the change. Form B10 is used for this purpose.

Remember, if you are notifying the appointment of a new director, the form must contain the signed consent of the appointee to the new position.

The Register of Secretaries

The Register of Secretaries must be kept at the company's registered office. It must be open to inspection by any shareholder without charge for at least two hours daily during business hours, and likewise by any other person, on payment of a fee not exceeding £1.00 (€1.27).

If the secretary is an individual, the Register must contain the following information:

- His or her present surname and forename and any former surnames and forenames
- His or her usual residential address
- Former names, as we saw earlier, are names which have been changed by deed poll, and do not include maiden names or nicknames.

If the secretary is a company, the register must specify:

- The secretary company's name
- The secretary company's registered office.

Changes of secretary or in the secretary's particulars must be notified to the Registrar of Companies within 14 days of the change. Form B10 is used for this purpose.

Remember, if you are notifying the appointment of a new secretary, the form must contain the signed consent of the appointee to the new position.

The Register of Directors' and Secretaries' Interests

Every director or secretary of the company is required to notify the company in writing of the fact that he or she has an interest in any company shares or debentures (which, loosely speaking, could be described as IOUs given by the company, and which commonly contain security over the assets of the company), and the number and class of those shares and debentures. He or she must also notify the company of the following within five days of the occurrenc:

- The occurrence of any event whereby he or she becomes interested in any such shares or debentures
- The occurrence of any event as a result of which he or she ceases to be interested in any of the shares or debentures
- The entering into of any contract to sell any such shares or debentures
- The assignment of any right granted to him or her to subscribe for shares or debentures in the company

With each new instance he or she must indicate the number and class of the debentures or shares concerned.

Note that these requirements also apply to "shadow directors". A shadow director, as noted earlier, is someone in accordance with whose instructions the directors of the company are accustomed to act.

A person has an interest for the purposes of these requirements when he or she is:

- A purchaser under a contract
- A beneficiary under a trust
- Entitled to exercise or control the exercise of rights, such as voting rights, which are attached to somebody else's shares or debentures
- Entitled to an option in respect of shares.

The interest of a spouse or child under 18 is treated as the interest of the director or secretary.

Every company must keep a register of these directors' and secretaries' interests in the shares or debentures of the company. The entries in the register against individual names must appear in chronological order. The register must be kept in the same place as the Register of Members, and open to inspection for at least two hours during business hours to members without charge or to others for a fee not exceeding 30p (€0.38). The register must be produced 15 minutes before any annual general meeting, and remain open to inspection by any member attending the meeting.

The Register of Debenture Holders

Earlier, debentures were described loosely as something akin to IOUs. Legally speaking, a debenture is a formal document which evidences a debt by the company to the debenture holder, and which contains a promise to repay the debt to the debenture holder. Nowadays, most debentures will also give some form of security to the debenture holder, for example a personal guarantee from one of the directors that he or she will repay the debt from his or her personal assets if the company defaults in repaying the debt. Another common form of security is the "charge" (see page 41), of which the mortgage is a type.

When borrowing money from a financial institution, the company will issue a single debenture in favour of the lender. However, it is also possible to raise money from private investors by issuing a series of debentures, that is the company "sells" a number of debentures, all carrying equal security rights, to members of the public or the investing community. This approach to raising finance is really only successful when the company has a high profile so that there will be a satisfactory market for the debentures.

A Register of Debenture Holders is only required to be kept by the company when it issues a series of debentures all carrying equal security rights. The Register must contain the name, address, and the amount of debentures held by each person holding debentures of the series, and must be available for inspection to members and creditors of the company for at least two hours daily during business hours without fee, or by any other person for a fee not exceeding 5p (€0.06).

Remember, there is no legal obligation to maintain a register of holders of single debentures, although, as a practical matter, it might prove convenient to have one anyway.

Registration of Charges

A charge is a right of security over an asset. This means that, if a company's fleet of vehicles is charged to secure the loan used to buy them, the vehicles may be taken by the lender and sold to recover the amounts owing, should the company default on its repayments. For example, a mortgage is a charge over land or property.

Under section 99 of the Companies Act 1963, details of all charges over the company's assets must be registered with the Register of Companies within 21 days of creation of the charge. The purpose of the section is to protect creditors and others who deal with the company by providing a public list that shows whether the company's assets are tied up as security or are available as security for new loans.

The Registrar of Companies cannot extend the 21 day time limit — that can only be done by the High Court. If a charge is not registered within the prescribed time limit, it is void, and cannot be enforced by the chargeholder. Understandably, most credit institutions take it upon themselves to ensure that the time limit is adhered to.

Copies of all instruments creating charges must be kept at the company's registered office and open to inspection for at least two hours by any creditor or member without fee.

A separate copy of Form 47 is used to register each charge.

Change of Registered Office

A company's registered office is its official "home". Any document delivered there is deemed in law to have been successfully delivered to the company. Therefore, those dealing with the company need:

- To know where the company's registered office is
- To be kept informed of any changes in location

- If the company changes its registered office, Form B2 notifying the change must be filed with the Registrar of Companies within 14 days of the change. The current filing fee is £10.00 (€12.70)
- A Register of Change of Registered Office, which records the various registered offices used by the company during its lifetime, may prove useful.

Accounting and Tax Requirements

The accounts and the audit

In exchange for the privilege of limited liability, the owners of a limited company are required to disclose, regularly and in a formal manner, certain financial information relating to the performance and condition of the company.

This information is contained in two sets of documents:

- The company's accounts
- The company's Annual Return.

Every limited company is obliged to keep proper books of account, which show :

- All money received and paid and the persons from whom it was received or to whom it was paid
- All sales and purchases
- All assets and liabilities.

In addition, the records of transactions should be kept in such a manner that accounts may be easily prepared from them. The accounts must be prepared at regular intervals. Usually, these intervals are annual although, exceptionally, periods of different lengths may be accounted for. These accounts are prepared by the directors, who take responsibility for them, and are presented to the shareholders at the Annual General Meeting.

The Companies Acts, 1963 - 1990 lay out the precise requirements for the presentation of the accounts and the information to be contained within them. In addition, Financial Reporting Standards (issued by the Accounting Standards Board in the UK and promulgated in Ireland by the Institute of Chartered Accountants In Ireland) and their predecessor documents, the Statements of Standard Accounting Practice issued by the major accounting bodies in the period 1970 - 1990, are binding on all accountants involved in the preparation or audit of accounts, and prescribe further disclosure and specific treatment of particular potentially contentious transactions (See *Accounting Standards: A Quick Reference, 3rd edition*, published by Oak Tree Press, ISBN 1 86076 050 3, paperback, price £9.95 (€12.63)).

To ensure that the accounts have been fairly prepared and presented, as well as complying with relevant legislation, an audit must be carried out. Independent accountants review:

- The company's systems of bookkeeping and accounting
- The compilation of the accounts
- The treatment of various transactions
- The preparation and presentation of the accounts.

They are required by legislation to state in their report, which forms part of the company's accounts, whether in their opinion:

- The accounts give a true and fair view of the company's affairs at the financial year end and of the profit or loss for the financial year
- The accounts give the information required by the Companies Acts, in the manner so required
- They have obtained all the information and explanations which, to the best of their knowledge and belief, were necessary for the purposes of the audit
- Proper books of accounts have been kept
- The company's balance sheet and profit and loss account are in agreement with the books of account
- Proper returns have been received from branches of the company not visited by them during the audit
- A financial situation, as specified in section 40, Companies Act 1983 (which requires the directors of a company to convene an Extraordinary General Meeting if the net assets of the company fall to half or less of the company's called up share capital) exists at the balance sheet date.

The preparation and presentation of company accounts and their audit are specialised areas and are not considered here.

For further information or advice, you are advised to consult your accountant. If you do not yet have an accountant, check the Golden Pages or contact one of the following accounting bodies:

> Association of Chartered Certified Accountants
> 9 Leeson Park, Dublin 6
> Tel: 01 496 3144
> Institute of Certified Public Accountants in Ireland
> 9 Ely Place, Dublin 2
> Tel: 01 676 7353
>
> Institute of Chartered Accountants in Ireland
> Chartered Accountants' House, 87-89 Pembroke Road, Dublin 4
> Tel: 01 668 0400

who will be happy to put you in touch with one of their members close to where you live.

In addition to satisfying legal requirements for disclosure of financial information, a company needs good accounting systems in order to provide management and the directors with information both to monitor company performance and to plan future development.

The company's Annual Return is part of the continuing administration of a limited company. Its completion and submission are the responsibility of the company's Secretary.

Taxation and the limited company

Since taxation planning is often a critical element in business success, it is essential that you discuss the taxation consequences and alternatives with your accountant, before forming a limited company.

If you do not yet have an accountant, check the Golden Pages or contact one of the bodies listed on the previous page.

You will have to register your newly formed company with the Revenue Commissioners for:

- Corporation Tax

- Value Added Tax, if your sales of goods or your supplies of services, if yours is a service business, is likely to exceed the relevant annual limits
- PAYE/PRSI, if your company intends to employ staff.

Forming a Company through an Agent

Having read through this book, you may feel that forming your own company yourself is just too much work or that you just don't have the time. You know what you want done and how to do it but you would rather that a professional, experienced in company formations, would take the task from you.

That's easy to arrange. The Golden Pages lists many of those who specialise in this work. They will take care of the paperwork and advise you on the various options open to you. Having read this book, you will be better informed and better able to make the right choices.

If you choose to use a company registration agent, you will need to decide whether you want a company formed specifically for your own purposes or whether a "ready made" company will do.

A purpose-made company

To have a company formed to your own requirements will involve the following steps:

- You must decide on the name and objects (in broad terms) of the company
- The agent will draft a suitable "objects" clause for your approval and will advise on the wording of the Memorandum and Articles of Association
- He will take care of the documentation and advise you once the company has been incorporated. (Remember, you cannot trade in the company's name until it has been incorporated and the first meeting of the Board of Directors has been held.)

The process of forming the company will take about six weeks. The fee will vary from agent to agent but expect to pay about £200 (€254).

A number of company registration agents, and others including accounting firms and solicitors, are participants in a scheme organised by the Companies Office that guarantees formation of private limited companies within ten days of the submission of the appropriate documentation. This fast turnaround — the norm is six weeks — is achieved by agreeing in advance with the Companies Office the text of a standard Memorandum and Articles of Association. All companies submitted for formation under this scheme must follow the standard agreed text, except in the primary objects clause. This reduces the amount of work the Companies Office staff must do in checking each company and allows for a speedy response.

A "ready-made" company

A ready-made company (the term "off the shelf" is often used, as agents have already formed these companies and simply take the file "off the shelf" in response to a client's request) is cheaper and is available for trading immediately (subject only to the first meeting of the Board of Directors).

The disadvantage with a ready-made company is that it will have been formed in a standard format and may not take into account your special requirements. In particular, the name of the company may be neither suitable nor acceptable.

To change a company name is not particularly difficult but it costs £50 (€63.49) in Companies Office fees and could take from two to six weeks. If you require the name of a ready-made company changed, you save very little in time or money over the cost of a purpose-formed company.

Checklist for forming a company through an agent

1 Decide whether your company is to be:
- Off the shelf
- Purpose made.

2 If the company is to be bought off the shelf:
- Are you happy with the name?
- Do you want it changed?
- Have you decided on an alternative?

3 If the company is to be purpose made to your requirements, are you clear on:
- A name?
- The objects (or at least what the company is to do in general terms)?
- How much the authorised and issued share capital of the company will be ?
- Whether there are any specific amendments you want to make to Table A?
- Who the subscribers will be and how many shares they will each take?
- Who the directors will be?
- Who the Secretary will be?
- Any other special requirements you may have?

From this information, a company registration agent will be able to proceed. Without it, you will waste most of your first meeting with the agent.

Appendix 1: Registrar of Companies

The Registrar of Companies is charged with the maintenance of records of documents filed by companies in accordance with the requirements of the Companies Acts.

The Registrar's address is:
The Registrar of Companies
Companies Registration Office
Parnell House
14 Parnell Square
Dublin 1.
Tel: 01 804 5200
Fax: 01 804 5222

The Companies Office is open to the public from 10.00 to 16.30 Monday to Friday (excluding Bank Holidays), though counter services are closed between 13.00 and 14.15 each day.

Summary of Filing Fees

Incorporation of an Irish company

	£	€
New Companies Registration Fee	50.00	63.49
Capital Duty (Minimum)*	1.00	1.27
Total	**51.00**	**64.76**

* *Capital duty is charged at a rate of one per cent of actual value of goods or assets contributed in return for shares in the company, less any liabilities which have been taken over or discharged by the company in consideration of that contribution, subject to a minimum of £1.00 (€1.27).*

	£	€
Form RBN1B: Registration of Business Name	25.00	31.74
Form B10: Notice of change of Director/Secretary or change in particulars of Director/Secretary	10.00	12.70
Form B2: Notice of change of Registered Office	10.00	12.70
Form B3: Notice of change in situation of Register of Members	10.00	12.70
Form 47: Registration of Charge	25.00	31.74
Change in Company Name	50.00	63.49

Appendix 2: Table A

Table A is the standard Articles of Association adopted by most companies. The following is reproduced from the Companies Act 1963, with annotations in bold. Draft your company's Articles of Association based on the following, with any amendments you feel are necessary (see section Articles of Association, page 19).

Table A

Part I
Regulations for management of a company limited by shares not being a private company.

Interpretation
1   In these regulations:
- "the Act" means the Companies Act, 1963 (No. 33 of 1963);
- "the directors" means the directors for the time being of the company or the directors present at a meeting of the board of directors and includes any person occupying the position of director by whatever name called;
- "the register" means the register of members to be kept as required by section 116 of the Act;
- "secretary" means any person appointed to perform the duties of the secretary of the company;
- "the office" means the registered office for the time being of the company;
- "the seal" means the common seal of the company.

> Expressions referring to writing shall, unless the contrary intention appears, be construed as including references to printing, lithography, photography and any other modes of representing or reproducing words in a visible form.
>   Unless the contrary intention appears, words or expressions contained in these regulations shall bear the same meaning as in

the Act or in any statutory modification thereof in force at the date at which these regulations become binding on the company.

Share capital and Variation of Rights

2 Without prejudice to any special rights previously conferred on the holders of any existing shares or class of shares, any share in the company may be issued with such preferred, deferred or other special rights or such restrictions, whether in regard to dividend, voting, return of capital or otherwise, as the company may from time to time by ordinary resolution determine.

3 If at any time the share capital is divided into different classes of shares, the rights attached to any class (unless otherwise provided by the terms of issue of the shares of that class) may, whether or not the company is being wound up, be varied or abrogated with the consent in writing of the holders of three-fourths of the issued shares of that class, or with the sanction of a special resolution passed at a separate general meeting of the holders of the shares of the class. To every such separate general meeting the provisions of these regulations relating to general meetings shall apply but so that the necessary quorum shall be two persons (one, in the case of a single-member company) at least holding or representing by proxy one-third of the issued shares of the class. If at any adjourned meeting of such holders a quorum as above defined is not present those members who are present shall be a quorum. Any holders of shares of the class present in person or by proxy may demand a poll.

4 The rights conferred upon the holders of the shares of any class issued with preferred or other rights shall not, unless otherwise expressly provided by the terms of issue of the shares of that class, be deemed to be varied by the creation or issue of further shares ranking pari passu therewith.

5 Subject to the provisions of these regulations relating to new shares, the shares shall be at the disposal of the directors, and they may (subject to the provisions of the Act) allot, grant options over or otherwise dispose of them to such persons, on such terms and

conditions and at such times as they may consider to be in the best interests of the company and its shareholders, but so that no share shall be issued at a discount, except in accordance with the provisions of the Act, and so that in the case of shares offered to the public for subscription, the amount payable on application on each share shall not be less than 5 per cent of the nominal amount of the share.
[This clause is to prevent the directors selling new shares in the company for less than their true value.]

6   *The company may exercise the powers of paying commissions conferred by section 59 of the Act, provided that the rate per cent. and the amount of the commission paid or agreed to be paid shall be disclosed in the manner required by that section, and the rate of the commission shall not exceed 10 per cent. of the price at which the shares in respect whereof the same is paid are issued or an amount equal to 10 per cent. of such price (as the case may be). Such commission may be satisfied by the payment of cash or the allotment of fully or partly paid shares or partly in one way and partly in the other. The company may also, on any issue of shares, pay such brokerage as may be lawful.*

7   *Except as required by law, no person shall be recognised by the company as holding shares upon any trust, and the company shall not be bound by or be compelled in any way to recognise (even when having notice thereof) any equitable, contingent, future or partial interest in any share or in any interest in any fractional part of a share or (except only as by these regulations or by law otherwise provided) any other rights in respect of any share except an absolute right to the entirety thereof in the registered holder: this shall not preclude the company from requiring the members or a transferee of shares to furnish the company with information as to the beneficial ownership of any share when such information is reasonably required by the company.*

8   *Every person whose name is entered as a member in the register shall be entitled without payment to receive within 2 months after allotment or lodgement of a transfer (or within such other period*

as the conditions of issue shall provide) one certificate for all his shares or several certificates each for one or more of his shares upon payment of 12.5p for every certificate after the first or such less sum as the directors shall from time to time determine, so, however, that in respect of a share or shares held jointly by several persons the company shall not be bound to issue more than one certificate, and delivery of a certificate for a share to one of several joint holders shall be sufficient delivery to all such holders. Every certificate shall be under seal and specify the shares to which it relates and the amount paid up thereon.

9   If a share certificate be defaced, lost or destroyed, it may be renewed on payment of 12.5p or such less sum and on such terms (if any) as to evidence and indemnity and the payment of out-of-pocket expenses of the company of investigating evidence as the directors think fit.

10 The company shall not give, whether directly or indirectly, and whether by means of a loan, guarantee, the provision of security or otherwise, any financial assistance for the purpose of or in connection with a purchase or subscription made or to be made by any person of or for any shares in the company or in its holding company, but this regulation shall not prohibit any transaction permitted by section 60 of the Act.

Lien

11 The company shall have a first and paramount lien on every share (not being a fully paid share) for all moneys (whether immediately payable or not) called or payable at a fixed time in respect of that share, and the company shall also have a first and paramount lien on all shares (other than fully paid shares) standing registered in the name of a single person for all moneys immediately payable by him or his estate to the company; but the directors may at any time declare the share to be wholly or in part exempt from the provision on this regulation. The company's lien on a share shall extend to all dividends payable thereon.

12   The company may sell, in such manner as the directors think fit, any shares on which the company has a lien, but no sale shall be made unless a sum in respect of which the lien exists is immediately payable, nor until the expiration of 14 days after a notice in writing, stating and demanding payment of such part of the amount in respect of which the lien exists as is immediately payable, has been given to the registered holder for the time being of the share, or the person entitled thereto by reason of his death or bankruptcy.

13   To give effect to any such sale, the directors may authorise some person to transfer the shares sold to the purchaser thereof. The purchaser shall be registered as the holder of the shares comprised in any such transfer, and he shall not be bound to see to the application of the purchase money, nor shall his title to the shares be affected by any irregularity or invalidity in the proceedings in reference to the sale.

14   The proceeds of the sale shall be received by the company and applied in payment of such part of the amount in respect of which the lien exists as is immediately payable, and the residue, if any, shall (subject to a like lien for sums not immediately payable as existed upon the shares before the sale) be paid to the person entitled to the shares at the date of the sale.

Calls on Shares

[Calls on shares occur when directors seek to bring in unpaid amounts on shares issued which were not fully paid up at the time of issue.]

15   The directors may from time to time make calls upon the members in respect of any moneys unpaid on their shares (whether on account of the nominal value of the shares or by way of premium) and not by the conditions of allotment thereof made payable at fixed times, provided that no call shall exceed one-fourth of the nominal value of the share or be payable at less than one month from the date fixed for the payment of the last preceding call, and each member shall (subject to receiving at least 14 days' notice specifying the time or times and place of payment) pay to the

company at the time or times and place so specified the amount called upon his shares. A call may be revoked or postponed as the directors may determine.

16   A call shall be deemed to have been made at the time when the resolution of the directors authorising the call was passed and may be required to be paid by instalments.

17   The joint holders of a share shall be jointly and severally liable to pay all calls in respect thereof.

18   If a sum called in respect of a share is not paid before or on the day appointed for payment thereof, the person from whom the sum is due shall pay interest on the sum from the day appointed for payment thereof to the time of actual payment at such rate, not exceeding 5 per cent. per annum, as the directors may determine, but the directors shall be at liberty to waive payment of such interest wholly or in part.

19   Any sum which by the terms of issue of a share becomes payable on allotment or at any fixed date, whether on account of the nominal value of the share or by way of premium, shall, for the purposes of these regulations, be deemed to be a call duly made and payable on the date which, by the terms of the issue, the same becomes payable, and in case of non-payment all the relevant provisions of these regulations as to payment of interest and expenses, forfeiture or otherwise, shall apply as if such sum had become payable by virtue of a call duly made and notified.

20   The directors may, on the issue of shares, differentiate between the holders as to the amount of calls to be paid and the times of payment.

21   The directors may, if they think fit, receive from any member willing to advance the same, all or any part of the moneys uncalled and unpaid upon any shares held by him, and upon all or any of the moneys so advanced may (until the same would, but for such advance, become payable) pay interest at such rate not ex-

ceeding (unless the company in general meeting otherwise directs) 5 per cent. per annum, as may be agreed upon between the directors and the member paying such sum in advance.

Transfer of Shares

22 The instrument of transfer of any share shall be executed by or on behalf of the transferor and transferee, and the transferor shall be deemed to remain the holder of the share until the name of the transferee is entered in the register in respect thereof.
[As indicated in the text (see page 36), it is the entry in the Register of Members (Share Register) that governs transfers not the transfer transaction itself.]

23 Subject to such of the restrictions of these regulations as may be applicable, any member may transfer all or any of his shares by instrument in writing in any usual or common form or any other form which the directors may approve.

24 The directors may decline to register the transfer of a share (not being a fully paid up share) to a person of whom they do not approve, and they may also decline to register the transfer of a share on which the company has a lien. The directors may also decline to register any transfer of a share which, in their opinion, may imperil or prejudicially affect the status of the company in the State or which may imperil any tax concession or rebate to which the members of the company may be entitled or which may involve the company in the payment of any additional stamp or other duties on any conveyance of any property made or to be made to the company.
[This clause gives directors rights over transfers designed to protect the company. However, if a prosepctive shareholder is, in his own view, unfairly denied a transfer of shares, he may take a case to the Courts to force the directors to register his transfer.]

25 The directors may also decline to recognise any instrument of transfer unless —

(a) a fee of 12.5p or such lesser sum as the directors may from time to time require, is paid to the company in respect thereof; and
(b) the instrument of transfer is accompanied by the certificate of the shares to which it relates, and such other evidence as the directors may reasonably require to show the right of the transferor to make the transfer; and
(c) The instrument of transfer is in respect of one class of share only.

26 If the directors refuse to register a transfer they shall, within 2 months after the date on which the transfer was lodged with the company, send to the transferee notice of the refusal.

27 The registration of transfers may be suspended at such times and for such periods, not exceeding in the whole 30 days in each year, as the directors may from time to time determine.

28 The company shall be entitled to charge a fee not exceeding 12.5p on the registration of every probate, letters of administration, certificate of death or marriage, power of attorney, notice as to stock or other instrument.

Transmission of shares

29 In the case of the death of a member, the survivor or survivors where the deceased was a joint holder, and the personal representatives of the deceased where he was a sole holder, shall be the only persons recognised by the company as having any title to his interest in the shares; but nothing herein contained shall release the estate of a deceased joint holder from any liability in respect of any share which had been jointly held by him with other persons.

30 Any person becoming entitled to a share in consequence of the death or bankruptcy of a member may, upon such evidence being produced as may from time to time properly be required by the directors and subject as hereinafter provided, elect either to be registered himself as the holder of the share or to have some other person nominated by him registered as the transferee thereof, but

the directors shall, in either case, have the same right to decline or suspend registration as they would have had in the case of a transfer of the share by that member before his death or bankruptcy, as that case may be.

31 *If the person so becoming entitled elects to be registered himself, he shall deliver or send to the company a notice in writing signed by him stating that he so elects. If he elects to have another person registered, he shall testify his election by executing to that person a transfer of the share. All the limitations, restrictions and provisions of these regulations relating to the right to transfer and the registration of transfers shall be applicable to any such notice or transfer as aforesaid as if the death or bankruptcy of the member had not occurred and the notice or transfer were a transfer signed by that member.*

32 *A person becoming entitled to a share by reason of the death or bankruptcy of the holder shall be entitled to the same dividends and other advantages to which he would be entitled if he were the registered holder of the share, except that he shall not, before being registered as a member in respect of the share, be entitled in respect of it to exercise any right conferred by membership in relation to meetings of the company, so, however, that the directors may at any time give notice requiring any such person to elect either to be registered himself or to transfer the share, and if the notice is not complied with within 90 days, the directors may thereupon withhold payment of all dividends, bonuses or other moneys payable in respect of the share until the requirements of the notice have been complied with.*

Forfeiture of shares

33 *If a member fails to pay any call or instalment of a call on the day appointed for payment thereof, the directors may, at any time thereafter during such time as any part of the call or instalment remains unpaid, serve a notice on him requiring payment of so much of the call or instalment as is unpaid together with any interest which may have accrued.*

34   The notice shall name a further day (not earlier than the expiration of 14 days from the date of service of the notice) on or before which the payment required by the notice is to be made, and shall state that in the event of non-payment at or before the time appointed the shares in respect of which the call was made will be liable to be forfeited.

35   If the requirements of any such notice as aforesaid are not complied with, any share in respect of which the notice has been given may at any time thereafter, before the payment required by the notice has been made, be forfeited by a resolution of the directors to that effect.

36   A forfeited share may be sold or otherwise disposed of on such terms and in such manner as the directors think fit, and at any time before a sale or disposition the forfeiture may be cancelled on such terms as the directors may think fit.

37   A person whose shares have been forfeited shall cease to be a member in respect of the forfeited shares, but shall, notwithstanding, remain liable to pay to the company all moneys which, at the date of forfeiture, were payable by him to the company in respect of the shares, but his liability shall cease if and when the company shall have received payment in full of all such moneys in respect of the shares.

38   A statutory declaration that the declarant is a director or the secretary of the company, and that a share in the company has been duly forfeited on a date stated in the declaration, shall be conclusive evidence of the facts therein stated as against all persons claiming to be entitled to the share. The company may receive the consideration, if any, given for the share on any sale or disposition thereof and may execute a transfer of the share in favour of the person to whom the share is sold or disposed of and he shall thereupon be registered as the holder of the share, and shall not be bound to see to the application of the purchase money, if any, nor shall his title to the share be affected by any irregularity or inva-

lidity in the proceedings in reference to the forfeiture, sale or disposal of the share.

39   The provisions of these regulations as to forfeiture shall apply in the case of non-payment of any sum which, by the terms of issue of a share, become payable at a fixed time, whether on account of the nominal value of the share or by way of premium, as if the same had been payable by virtue of a call duly made and notified.

Conversion of Shares into Stock

40   The company may by ordinary resolution convert any paid up shares into stock, and reconvert any stock into paid up shares of any denomination.

41   The holders of stock may transfer the same, or any part thereof, in the same manner, and subject to the same regulations, as and subject to which the shares from which the stock arose might previously to conversion have been transferred, or as near thereto as circumstances admit; and the directors may from time to time fix the minimum amount of stock transferable but so that such minimum shall not exceed the nominal amount of each share from which the stock arose.

42   The holders of stock shall, according to the amount of stock held by them, have the same rights, privileges and advantages in relation to dividends, voting at meetings of the company and other matters as if they held the shares from which the stock arose, but no such right, privilege or advantage (except participation in the dividends and profits of the company and in the assets on winding up) shall be conferred by an amount of stock which would not, if existing in shares, have conferred that right, privilege or advantage.

43   Such of the regulations of the company as are applicable to paid up shares shall apply to stock, and the words "share" and "shareholder" therein shall include "stock" and "stockholder".

Alteration of Capital

44   The company may from time to time by ordinary resolution increase the share capital by such sum, to be divided into shares of such amount, as the resolution shall prescribe.

45   The company may by ordinary resolution —
 (a)   consolidate and divide all or any of its share capital into shares of larger amount than its existing shares;
 (b)   subdivide its existing shares, or any of them, into shares of smaller amount than is fixed by the memorandum of association subject, nevertheless, to section 69 (1)(d) of the Act;
 (c)   cancel any shares which, at the date of the passing of the resolution, have not been taken or agreed to be taken by any person.

46   The company may by special resolution reduce its share capital, any capital redemption reserve fund or any share premium account in any manner and with and subject to any incident authorised, and consent required, by law.

General meetings

47   All general meetings of the company shall be held in the State.

48   (1)   Subject to paragraph (2) of this regulation, the company shall in each year hold a general meeting as its annual general meeting in addition to any other meeting in that year, and shall specify the meeting as such in the notices calling it; and not more than 15 months shall elapse between the date of one annual general meeting and that of the next.
 (2)   So long as the company holds its first annual general meeting within 18 months of its incorporation, it need not hold it in the year of its incorporation or in the year following. Subject to regulation 47, the annual general meeting shall be held at such time and place as the directors shall appoint.

49   All general meetings other than annual general meetings shall be called extraordinary general meetings.

50 *The directors may, whenever they think fit, convene an extraordinary general meeting, and extraordinary general meetings may be convened on such requisition, or in default, may be convened by such requisitionists, as provided by section 132 of the Act. If at any time there are not within the State sufficient directors capable of acting to form a quorum, any director or any 2 members (one, in the case of a single-member company) of the company may convene an extraordinary general meeting in the same manner as nearly as possible as that in which meetings may be convened by the directors.*

Notice of General Meetings

51 *Subject to sections 133 and 141 of the Act, an annual general meeting and a meeting called for the passing of a special resolution shall be called by 21 days' notice in writing at least, and a meeting of the company (other than an annual general meeting or a meeting for the passing of a special resolution) shall be called by 14 days' notice in writing at the least. The notice shall be exclusive of the day on which it is served or deemed to be served and of the day for which it is given, and shall specify the place, the day and the hour of the meeting, and in the case of special business, the general nature of that business, and shall be given, in the manner hereinafter mentioned, to such persons as are, under the regulations of the company, entitled to receive such notices from the company.*

52 *The accidental omission to give notice of a meeting to, or the non-receipt of notice of a meeting by, any person entitled to receive notice shall not invalidate the proceedings at the meeting.*

Proceedings at General Meetings

53 *All business shall be deemed special that is transacted at an extraordinary general meeting, and also all that is transacted at an annual general meeting, with the exception of declaring a dividend, the consideration of the accounts, balance sheets and the reports of the directors and auditors, the election of directors in place of those retiring, the re-appointment of the retiring auditors and the fixing of the remuneration of the auditors.*

54	No business shall be transacted at any general meeting unless a quorum of members is present at the time when the meeting proceeds to business; save as herein otherwise provided, three members (one, in the case of a single-member company) present in person shall be a quorum.

55	If within half an hour from the time appointed for the meeting a quorum is not present, the meeting, if convened upon the requisition of members, shall be dissolved; in any other case it shall stand adjourned to the same day in the next week, at the same time and place or to such other day and at such other time and place as the directors may determine, and if at the adjourned meeting a quorum is not present within half an hour from the time appointed for the meeting, the members present shall be a quorum.

56	The chairman, if any, of the board of directors shall preside as chairman at every general meeting of the company, or if there is no such chairman, or if he is not present within 15 minutes after the time appointed for the holding of the meeting or is unwilling to act, the directors present shall elect one of their number to be chairman of the meeting.

57	If at any meeting no director is willing to act as chairman or if no director is present within 15 minutes after the time appointed for holding the meeting, the members present shall choose one of their number to be chairman of the meeting.

58	The chairman may, with the consent of any meeting at which a quorum is present, and shall if so directed by the meeting, adjourn the meeting from time to time and from place to place, but no business shall be transacted at any adjourned meeting other than the business left unfinished at the meeting from which the adjournment took place. When a meeting is adjourned for 30 days or more, notice of the adjourned meeting shall be given as in the case of an original meeting. Save as aforesaid it shall not be necessary to give notice of an adjournment or of the business to be transacted at an adjourned meeting.

59 At any general meeting a resolution put to the vote of the meeting shall be decided on a show of hands unless a poll is (before or on the declaration of the result of the show of hands) demanded
   (a)   by the chairman; or
   (b)   by at least three members present in person or by proxy; or
   (c)   by any member or members present in person or by proxy and representing not less than one-tenth of the total voting rights of all the members having the right to vote at the meeting; or
   (d)   by a member or members holding shares in the company conferring the right to vote at the meeting being shares on which an aggregate sum has been paid up equal to not less than one-tenth of the total sum paid up on all the shares conferring that right.

   Unless a poll is so demanded, a declaration by the chairman that a resolution has, on a show of hands, been carried or carried unanimously, or by a particular majority, or lost, and an entry to that effect in the book containing the minutes of the proceedings of the company shall be conclusive evidence of the fact without proof of the number or proportion of the votes recorded in favour or against such resolution.
   The demand for a poll may be withdrawn.

60 Except as provided in regulation 62, if a poll is duly demanded it shall be taken in such manner as the chairman directs, and the result of the poll shall be deemed to be the resolution of the meeting at which the poll was demanded.

61 Where there is an equality of votes, whether on a show of hands or on a poll, the chairman of the meeting at which the show of hands takes place or at which the poll is demanded, shall be entitled to a second or casting vote.

62 A poll demanded on the election of a chairman or on a question of adjournment shall be taken forthwith. A poll demanded on any other question shall be taken at such time as the chairman of the

meeting directs, and any business other than that on which a poll is demanded may be proceeded with pending the taking of the poll.

Votes of Members

63   *Subject to any rights or restrictions for the time being attached to any class or classes of shares, on a show of hands every member present in person and every proxy shall have one vote, so, however, that no individual shall have more than one vote, and on a poll every member shall have one vote for each share of which he is the holder.*

64   *Where there are joint holders, the vote of the senior who tenders a vote, whether in person or by proxy, shall be accepted to the exclusion of the votes of the other joint holders; and for this purpose, seniority shall be determined by the order in which the names stand in the register.*

65   *A member of unsound mind, or in respect of whom an order has been made by any court having jurisdiction in lunacy, may vote, whether on a show of hands or on a poll, by his committee, receiver, guardian or other person appointed by that court, and any such committee, receiver, guardian or other person may vote by proxy on a show of hands or on a poll.*

66   *No member shall be entitled to vote at any general meeting unless all calls or other sums immediately payable by him in respect of shares in the company have been paid.*

67   *No objection shall be raised to the qualification of any voter except at the meeting or adjourned meeting at which the vote objected to is given or tendered, and every vote not disallowed at such meeting shall be valid for all purposes. Any such objection made in due time shall be referred to the chairman of the meeting, whose decision shall be final and conclusive.*

68   *Votes may be given either personally or by proxy.*

69 The instrument appointing a proxy shall be in writing under the hand of the appointer or of his attorney duly authorised in writing, or, if the appointer is a body corporate, either under seal or under the hand of an officer or attorney duly authorised. A proxy need not be a member of the company.

70 The instrument appointing a proxy and the power of attorney or other authority, if any, under which it is signed, or a notarially certified copy of that power or authority shall be deposited at the office or at such other place within the State as is specified for that purpose in the notice convening the meeting, not less than 48 hours before the time for holding the meeting or adjourned meeting at which the person named in the instrument proposes to vote, or, in the case of a poll, not less than 48 hours before the time appointed for the taking of the poll, and, in the default, the instrument of proxy shall not be treated as valid.

71 An instrument appointing a proxy shall be in the following form or a form as near thereto as circumstances permit —
(Company name) Limited.
I/We of ..... in the County of ..... , being a member/members of the above-named company hereby appoint ..... of ..... or failing him, ... of ..... as my/our proxy to vote for me/us on my/our behalf at the (annual or extraordinary, as the case may be) general meeting of the company to be held on the ..... day of ..... , 20.. and at any adjournment thereof.
Signed this ..... day of ..... , 20..
(Signature)
This form is to be used *in favour of/against the resolution.
Unless otherwise instructed the proxy will vote as he thinks fit.
* Strike out whichever is not desired.

72 The instrument appointing a proxy shall be deemed to confer authority to demand or join in demanding a poll.

73   A vote given in accordance with the terms of an instrument of proxy shall be valid notwithstanding the previous death or insanity of the principal or revocation of the proxy or of the authority under which the proxy was executed or of the transfer of the share in respect of which the proxy is given, if no intimation in writing of such death, insanity, revocation or transfer as aforesaid is received by the company at the office before the commencement of the meeting or adjourned meeting at which the proxy is used.

Bodies Corporate acting by Representatives at Meetings

74   Any body corporate which is a member of the company may, by resolution of its directors or other governing body, authorise such person as it thinks fit to act as its representative at any meeting of the company or of any class of members of the company, and the person so authorised shall be entitled to exercise the same powers on behalf of the body corporate which he represents as that body corporate could exercise if it were an individual member of the company.

The Directors

75   The number of directors and the names of the first directors shall be determined in writing by the subscriber(s) of the memorandum of association or a majority of them.

76   The remuneration of the directors shall from time to time be determined by the company in general meeting. Such remuneration shall be deemed to accrue from day to day. The directors may also be paid all travelling, hotel and other expenses properly incurred by them in attending and returning from meetings of the directors or any committee of the directors or general meetings of the company or in connection with the business of the company.

77   The share holding qualification for directors may be fixed by the company in general meeting and, unless and until so fixed, no qualification shall be required.
     [Sometimes, companies demand that directors each hold a minimum number of shares as an expression of their own commitment to the company.]

78 A director of the company may be or become a director or other officer of, or otherwise interested in, any company promoted by the company or in which the company may be interested as shareholder or otherwise, and no such director shall be accountable to the company for any remuneration or other benefits received by him as a director or officer of, or from his interest in, such other company unless the company otherwise directs.

Borrowing Powers

79 The directors may exercise all the powers of the company to borrow money, and to mortgage or charge its undertaking, property and uncalled capital, or any part thereof, and to issue debentures, debenture stock and other securities, whether outright or as security for any debt, liability or obligation of the company or of any third party, so, however, that the amount for the time being remaining undischarged of moneys borrowed or secured by the directors as aforesaid (apart from temporary loans obtained from the company's bankers in the ordinary course of business) shall not at any time, without the previous sanction of the company in general meeting, exceed the nominal amount of the share capital of the company for the time being issued, but nevertheless no lender or other person dealing with the company shall be concerned to see or inquire whether this limit is observed. No debt incurred or security given in excess of such limit shall be invalid or ineffectual except in the case of express notice to the lender or the recipient of the security at the time when the debt was incurred or security given that the limit had been or was thereby exceeded.

Powers and Duties of Directors

80 The business of the company shall be managed by the directors, who may pay all expenses incurred in promoting and registering the company and may exercise all such powers of the company as are not, by the Act or by these regulations, required to be exercised by the company in general meeting, subject, nevertheless, to any of these regulations, to the provisions of the Act and to such directions, being not inconsistent with the aforesaid regulations or provisions, as may be given by the company in general meeting; but no direction given by the company in general meeting

shall invalidate any prior act of the directors which would have been valid if that direction had not been given.

81   The directors may from time to time and at any time by power of attorney appoint any company, firm or person or body of persons, whether nominated directly or indirectly by the directors, to be the attorney or attorneys of the company for such purposes and with such powers, authorities and discretions (not exceeding those vested in or exercisable by the directors under these regulations) and for such period and subject to such conditions as they may think fit, and any such power of attorney may contain such provisions for the protection of persons dealing with any such attorney as the directors may think fit, and may also authorise any such attorney to delegate all or any of the powers, authorities and discretions vested in him.

82   The company may exercise the powers conferred by section 41 of the Act with regard to having an official seal for use abroad, and such powers shall be vested in the directors.

83   A director who is in any way, whether directly or indirectly, interested in a contract or proposed contract with the company shall declare the nature of his interest at a meeting of the directors in accordance with section 194 of the Act.

84   A director shall not vote in respect of any contract or arrangement in which he is so interested, and if he shall so vote, his vote shall not be counted, nor shall he be counted in the quorum present at the meeting but neither of these prohibitions shall apply to
   (a)   any arrangement for giving any director any security or indemnity in respect of money lent by him to or obligation undertaken by him for the benefit of the company; or
   (b)   any arrangement for the giving by the company of any security to a third party in respect of a debt or an obligation of the company for which the director himself has assumed responsibility in whole or in part under a guarantee or indemnity or by the deposit of a security; or

(c) any contract by a director to subscribe for or underwrite shares or debentures of the company; or

(d) any contract or arrangement with any other company in which he is interested only as an officer of such other company or as a holder of shares or other securities in such other company;

and these prohibitions may at any time be suspended or relaxed to any extent and either generally or in respect of any particular contract, arrangement or transaction by the company in general meeting.

[Paragraphs 83 and 84 are designed to identify and prevent conflicts of interests between a director's role within the company and his other activities.]

85 A director may hold any other office or place of profit under the company (other than the office of auditor) in conjunction with his office of director for such period and on such terms as to remuneration and otherwise as the directors may determine, and no director or intending director shall be disqualified by his office from contracting with the company either with regard to his tenure of any such other office or place of profit as vendor, purchaser or otherwise, nor shall any such contract or arrangement entered into by or on behalf of the company in which any director is in any way interested, be liable to be avoided, nor shall any director so contracting or being so interested be liable to account to the company for any profit realised by any such contract or arrangement by reason of such director holding that office or of the fiduciary relation thereby established.

86 A director, notwithstanding his interest, may be counted in the quorum present at any meeting whereat he or any other director is appointed to hold such office or place or profit under the company or whereat the terms of any such appointment are arranged, and he may vote on any such appointment or arrangement other than his own appointment or the arrangement of the terms thereof.

87 Any director may act by himself or his firm in a professional capacity for the company, and he or his firm shall be entitled to

remuneration for professional services as if he were not a director; but nothing herein contained shall authorise a director or his firm to act as auditor to the company.

88 All cheques, promissory notes, drafts, bills of exchange and other negotiable instruments and all receipts for moneys paid to the company shall be signed, drawn, accepted, endorsed or otherwise executed, as the case may be, by such person or persons and in such manner as the directors shall from time to time by resolution determine.

89 The directors shall cause minutes to be made in books provided for the purpose
    (a)   of all appointments of officers made by directors;
    (b)   of the names of all directors present at each meeting of the directors and of any committee of the directors;
    (c)   of all resolutions and proceedings at all meetings of the company and of the directors and of committees of the directors.

[This record of directors' appointments, attendance and decisions at meetings reflects their role as stewards of the company and its assets on behalf of the shareholders.]

90 The directors on behalf of the company may pay a gratuity or pension or allowance on retirement to any director who has held any other salaried office or place of profit with the company or to his widow or dependents, and may make contributions to any fund and pay premiums for the purchase or provision of any such gratuity, pension or allowance.

Disqualification of Directors

91 The office of director shall be vacated if the director —
    (a)   ceases to be a director by virtue of section 180 of the Act; or
    (b)   is adjudged bankrupt in the State or in Northern Ireland or Great Britain or makes any arrangement or composition with his creditors generally; or
    (c)   becomes prohibited from being a director by reason of any order made under section 184 of the Act; or

(d) becomes of unsound mind;
(e) resigns his office by notice in writing to the company; or
(f) is convicted of an indictable offence unless the directors otherwise determine; or
(g) is more than 6 months absent without permission of the directors from meetings of the directors held during that period.

Rotation of Directors

92 *At the first annual general meeting of the company all the directors shall retire from office, and at the annual general meeting in every subsequent year, one-third of the directors for the time being, or, if their number is not three or a multiple of three, then the number nearest one-third shall retire from office.*

[In family companies, where all the directors are shareholders, it is common to delete this paragraph, thus avoiding the need for directors to resign and be re-elected.]

93 *The directors to retire in every year shall be those who have been longest in office since their last election but as between persons who became directors on the same day, those to retire shall (unless they otherwise agree among themselves) be determined by lot.*

94 *A retiring director shall be eligible for re-election.*

95 *The company, at the meeting at which a director retires in the manner aforesaid, may fill the vacated office by electing a person thereto, and in default the retiring director shall, if offering himself for re-election, be deemed to have been re-elected, unless at such meeting it is expressly resolved not to fill such vacated office, or unless a resolution for the re-election of such director has been put to the meeting and lost.*

96 *No person other than a director retiring at the meeting shall, unless recommended by the directors, be eligible for election to the office of director at any general meeting unless not less than 3 nor more than 21 days before the day appointed for the meeting there shall have been left at the office notice in writing signed by a*

member duly qualified to attend and vote at the meeting for which such notice is given, of his intention to propose such person for election and also notice in writing signed by that person of his willingness to be elected.

97 The company may from time to time by ordinary resolution increase or reduce the number of directors and may also determine in what rotation the increased or reduced number is to go out of office.

98 The directors shall have power at any time and from time to time to appoint any person to be a director, either to fill a casual vacancy or as an addition to the existing directors, but so that the total number of directors shall not at any time exceed the number fixed in accordance with these regulations. Any director so appointed shall hold office only until the next following annual general meeting, and shall then be eligible for re-election but shall not be taken into account in determining the directors who are to retire by rotation at such meeting.

99 The company may, by ordinary resolution, of which extended notice has been given in accordance with section 142 of the Act, remove any director before the expiration of his period of office notwithstanding anything in these regulations or in any agreement between the company and such director. Such removal shall be without prejudice to any claim such director may have for breach of contract of service between him and the company.

100 The company may, by ordinary resolution, appoint another person in place of a director removed from office under regulation 99 and, without prejudice to the powers of the directors under regulation 98, the company in general meeting may appoint any person to be a director either to fill a casual vacancy or as an additional director. A person appointed in place of a director so removed or to fill such vacancy shall be subject to retirement at the same time as if he had become a director on the day on which the director in whose place he is appointed was last elected a director.

Proceedings of Directors

101 The directors may meet together for despatch of business, adjourn and otherwise regulate their meetings as they think fit. Questions arising at any meeting shall be decided by a majority of votes. Where there is an equality of votes, the chairman shall have a second or casting vote. A director may, and the secretary on the requisition of a director shall, at any time, summon a meeting of the directors. If the directors so resolve, it shall not be necessary to give notice of a meeting of directors to any director, who being resident in the State, is for the time being absent from the State.

102 The quorum necessary for the transaction of the business of the directors may be fixed by the directors, and unless so fixed shall be two.

103 The continuing directors may act notwithstanding any vacancy in their number but, if and so long as their number is reduced below the number fixed or pursuant to the regulations of the company as the necessary quorum of directors, the continuing directors or director may act for the purpose of increasing the number of directors to that number or of summoning a general meeting of the company but for no other purpose.

104 The directors may elect a chairman of their meetings and determine the period for which he is to hold office, but if no such chairman is elected, or, if at any meeting the chairman is not present within 5 minutes after the time appointed for holding the same, the directors present may choose one of their number to be the chairman of the meeting.

105 The directors may delegate any of their powers to committees consisting of such member or members of the board as they think fit; any committee so formed shall, in the exercise of the powers so delegated, conform to any regulations that may be imposed on it by the directors.

106 A committee may elect a chairman of its meetings; if no such chairman is elected, or if at any meeting the chairman is not pres-

ent within 5 minutes after the time appointed for holding the same, the members present may choose one of their number to be chairman of the meeting.

107 A committee may meet and adjourn as it thinks proper. Questions arising at any meeting shall be determined by a majority of votes of the members present, and where there is an equality of votes, the chairman shall have a second or casting vote.

108 All acts done by any meeting of the directors or by a committee of the directors or by any person acting as a director shall, notwithstanding that it be afterwards discovered that there was some defect in the appointment of any such director or person acting as aforesaid, or that they or any of them were disqualified, be as valid as if every person had been duly appointed and was qualified to be a director.

109 A resolution in writing signed by all the directors for the time being entitled to receive notice of a meeting of the directors shall be as valid as if it had been passed at a meeting of the directors duly convened and held.
[**This paragraph is important as it avoids the need for directors to be physically present at a meeting of the directors. The safeguard is that all directors must sign the resolution.**]

Managing Director

110 The directors may from time to time appoint one or more of themselves to the office of managing director for such period and on such terms as to remuneration and otherwise as they think fit, and, subject to the terms of any agreement entered into in any particular case, may revoke such appointment. A director so appointed shall not, whilst holding that office, be subject to retirement by rotation or be taken into account in determining the rotation of retirement of directors but (without prejudice to any claim he may have for damages for breach of any contract of service between him and the company), his appointment shall be automatically determined if he ceases from any cause to be a director.

111   A managing director shall receive such remuneration whether by salary, commission or participation in the profits, or partly in one way and partly in another, as the directors may determine.

112   The directors may entrust to and confer upon a managing director any of the powers exercisable by them upon such terms and conditions and with such restrictions as they think fit, and either collaterally with or to the exclusion of their own powers, and may from time to time revoke, alter or vary all or any of such powers.

The Secretary

113   The secretary shall be appointed by the directors for such term, at such remuneration and upon such conditions as they may think fit; and any such secretary so appointed may be removed by them.

114   A provision of the Act or these regulations requiring or authorising a thing to be done by a director and the secretary shall not be satisfied by its being done by or to the same person acting both as director and as, or in place of, the secretary.
[Although one person can be both secretary and a director, when the signatures of both the secretary and a director are required, he cannot act in both roles for the purposes of signing. This prevents concentration of too much authority in one person's hands.]

The Seal

115   The seal shall be used only by the authority of the directors or of a committee of directors authorised by the directors in that behalf, and every instrument to which the seal shall be affixed shall be signed by a director and shall be countersigned by the secretary or by a second director or by some other person appointed by the directors for the purpose.

Dividends and Reserves

116   The company in general meeting may declare dividends, but no dividend shall exceed the amount recommended by the directors.

[It is the shareholders who declare dividends but they must be guided by the directors who are stewards of the company.]

117 The directors may from time to time pay to the members such interim dividends as appear to the directors to be justified by the profits of the company.

118 No dividend shall be paid otherwise than out of profits.

119 The directors may, before recommending any dividend, set aside out of the profits of the company such sums as they think proper as a reserve or reserves which shall, at the discretion of the directors, be applicable for any purpose to which the profits of the company may be properly applied, and pending such application may, at the like discretion, either be employed in the business of the company or be invested in such investments as the directors may lawfully determine. The directors may also, without placing the same to reserve, carry forward any profits which they may think it prudent not to divide.

120 Subject to the rights of persons, if any, entitled to shares with special rights as to dividend, all dividends shall be declared and paid according to the amounts paid or credited as paid on the shares in respect whereof the dividend is paid, but no amount paid or credited as paid on a share in advance of calls shall be treated for the purposes of this regulation as paid on the share. All dividends shall be apportioned and paid proportionately to the amounts paid or credited as paid on the shares during any portion or portions of the period in respect of which the dividend is paid; but if any share is issued on terms providing that it shall rank for dividend as from a particular date, such share shall rank accordingly.

121 The directors may deduct from any dividend payable to any member all sums of money (if any) immediately payable by him to the company on account of calls or otherwise in relation to the shares of the company.

122 *Any general meeting declaring a dividend or bonus may direct payment of such dividend or bonus wholly or partly by the distribution of specific assets and in particular of paid up shares, debentures or debenture stock of any other company or in any one or more of such ways, and the directors shall give effect to such resolution, and where any difficulty arises in regard to such distribution, the directors may settle the same as they think expedient, and in particular may issue fractional certificates and fix the value for distribution of such specific assets or any part thereof and may determine that cash payments shall be made to members upon the footing of the value so fixed, in order to adjust the rights of all the parties, and may vest any such specific assets in trustees as may seem expedient to the directors.*

123 *Any dividend, interest or other moneys payable in cash in respect of any shares may be paid by cheque or warrant sent through the post directed to the registered address of the holder, or, where there are joint holders, to the registered address of that one of the joint holders who is first named on the register or to such person and to such address as the holder or joint holders may in writing direct. Every such cheque or warrant shall be made payable to the order of the person to whom it is sent. Any one of the two or more joint holders may give effectual receipts for any dividends, bonuses or other moneys payable in respect of the shares held by them as joint holders.*

124 *No dividend shall bear interest against the company.*

Accounts

125 *The directors shall cause proper books of account to be kept relating to —*
    (a)   all sums of money received and expended by the company and the matters in respect of which the receipt and expenditure takes place; and
    (b)   all sales and purchases of goods by the company; and
    (c)   the assets and liabilities of the company.

Proper books shall not be deemed to be kept if there are not kept such books of account as are necessary to give a true and fair view of the company's state of affairs and to explain its transactions.

126 The books of account shall be kept at the office or, subject to section 147 of the Act, at such other place as the directors think fit, and shall at all reasonable time be open to the inspection of the directors.

127 The directors shall from time to time determine whether and to what extent and at what times and places and under what conditions or regulations the accounts and books of the company or any of them shall be open to the inspection of members, not being directors, and no member (not being a director) shall have any right of inspecting any account or book or document of the company except as conferred by statute or authorised by the directors or by the company in general meeting.

128 The directors shall from time to time, in accordance with sections 148, 150, 157 and 158 of the Act cause to be prepared and to be laid before the annual general meeting of the company such profit and loss accounts, balance sheets, group accounts and reports as are required by those sections to be prepared and laid before the annual general meeting of the company.

129 A copy of every balance sheet (including every document required by law to be annexed thereto) which is to be laid before the annual general meeting of the company together with a copy of the directors' report and auditors' report shall, not less than 21 days before the date of the annual general meeting be sent to every person entitled under the provisions of the Act to receive them.

Capitalisation of Profits

130 The company in general meeting may upon the recommendation of the directors resolve that any sum for the time being standing to the credit of any of the company's reserves (including any capital redemption reserve fund or share premium account) or to the credit of profit and loss account be capitalised and applied on be-

half of the members who would have been entitled to receive the same if the same had been distributed by way of dividend and in the same proportions either in or towards paying up amounts for the time unpaid on any shares held by them respectively or in paying up full unissued shares or debentures of the company of a nominal amount equal to the sum capitalised (such shares or debentures to be allotted and distributed credited as fully paid up to and amongst such holders in the proportions aforesaid) or partly in one way and partly in another, so however, that the only purpose for which sums standing to the credit of the capital redemption reserve fund or the share premium account shall be applied shall be those permitted by sections 62 and 64 of the Act.

131 *Whenever such a resolution aforesaid shall have been passed, the directors shall make all appropriations and applications of the undivided profits resolved to be capitalised thereby and all allotments and issues of fully paid shares or debentures, if any, and generally shall do all acts and things required to give effect thereto with full power to the directors to make such provision as they shall think fit for the case of shares or debentures becoming distributable in fractions (and, in particular, without prejudice to the generality of the foregoing, to sell the shares or debentures represented by such fractions and distribute the net proceeds of such sale amongst the members otherwise entitled to such fractions in due proportions) and also to authorise any persons to enter on behalf of all of the members concerned into an agreement with the company providing for the allotment to them respectively credited as fully paid up of any further shares or debentures to which they may become entitled on such capitalisation or, as the case may require, for the payment up by the application thereto of their respective proportions of the profits resolved to be capitalised remaining unpaid on their existing shares and any agreement made under such authority shall be effective and binding on all such members.*

Audit

132 *Auditors shall be appointed and their duties regulated in accordance with sections 160 to 163 of the Act.*

Notices

133 A notice may be given by the company to any member either personally or by sending it by post to him to his registered address. Where a notice is sent by post, service of the notice shall be deemed to be effected by properly addressing, prepaying and posting a letter containing the notice, and to have been effected in the case of a notice of a meeting at the expiration of 24 hours after the letter containing the same is posted, and in any other case at the time at which the letter would be delivered in the ordinary course of post.

134 A notice may be given by the company to the joint holders of a share by giving the notice to the joint holder first named in the register in respect of the share.

135 A notice may be given by the company to the persons entitled to a share in consequence of the death or bankruptcy of a member by sending it through the post in a prepaid letter addressed to them by name or by the title of representatives of the deceased or Official Assignee in bankruptcy or by any like description at the address supplied for the purpose by the persons claiming to be so entitled, or (until such an address has been so supplied) by giving the notice in any manner in which the same might have been given if the death or bankruptcy had not occurred.

136 Notice of every general meeting shall be given in any manner hereinbefore authorised to
    (a)   every member; and
    (b)   every person upon whom the ownership of a share devolves by reason of his being a personal representative of the Official Assignee in bankruptcy of a member, where the member but for his death or bankruptcy would be entitled to receive notice of the meeting; and
    (c)   the auditor for the time being of the company.

No other person shall be entitled to receive notices of general meetings.

Winding Up

137   If the company is wound up, the liquidator may, with the sanction of a special resolution of the company and any other sanction required by the Act, divide among the members in specie or in kind the whole or any part of the assets of the company (whether they shall consist of property of the same kind or not) and may, for such purpose set such value as he deems fair upon any property to be divided as aforesaid and may determine how such division shall be carried out as between the members of different classes of members. The liquidator may, with the like sanction, vest the whole or any part of such assets in trustees upon such trusts for the benefit of the contributories as the liquidator, with the like sanction, shall think fit, but so that no member shall be compelled to accept any shares or other securities whereon there is any liability.

Indemnity

138   Every director, managing director, agent, auditor, secretary and other officer for the time being of the company shall be indemnified out of the assets of the company against any liability incurred by him in defending any proceedings, whether civil or criminal, in relation to his acts while acting in such office, in which judgement is given in his favour or in which he is acquitted or in connection with any application under section 391 of the Act in which relief is granted to him by the court.

Part II
Regulations for the Management of a Private Company Limited by Shares
[The Companies Act 1963 includes these amendments to Table A, Part I to reflect the special needs of private companies.]

1   The regulations contained in Part I of Table A (with the exception of regulations 24, 51, 54, 84 and 86) shall apply.

2   The company is a private company and accordingly —
   (a)   the right to transfer shares is restricted in the manner hereinafter prescribed;

(b) the number of members of the company (exclusive of persons who are in the employment of the company and of persons who, having formerly been in the employment of the company, were while in such employment, and have continued after the determination of such employment to be, members of the company) is limited to fifty, so, however, that where two or more persons hold one or more shares in the company jointly, they shall, for the purpose of this regulation, be treated as a single member.

(c) any invitation to the public to subscribe for any shares or debentures of the company is prohibited;

(d) the company shall not have the power to issue share warrants to bearer.

3 The directors may, in their absolute discretion, and without assigning any reason therefor, decline to register any transfer of any share, whether or not it is a fully paid share.
[This is a valuable and important right of the directors, often used to protect the company from unwelcome takeovers.]

4 Subject to sections 133 and 141 of the Act, an annual general meeting and a meeting called for the passing of a special resolution shall be called by 21 days' notice in writing at the least and a meeting of the company (other than an annual general meeting or a meeting for the passing of a special resolution) shall be called by 7 days' notice in writing at the least. The notice shall be exclusive of the day on which it is served or deemed to be served and of the day for which it is given and shall specify the day, the place and the hour of the meeting and, in the case of special business, the general nature of that business and shall be given in manner authorised by these regulations to such persons as are under the regulations of the company entitled to receive such notices from the company.

5 No business shall be transacted at any general meeting unless a quorum of members is present at the time when the meeting pro-

ceeds to business; save as herein otherwise provided, two members present in person or by proxy shall be a quorum.

6 *Subject to section 141 of the Act, a resolution in writing signed by all the members for the time being entitled to attend and vote on such resolution at a general meeting (or being bodies corporate by their duly authorised representatives) shall be as valid and effective for all purposes as if the resolution had been passed at a general meeting of the company duly convened and held, and if described as a special resolution shall be deemed to be a special resolution within the meaning of the Act.*
[Again, this paragraph gives the facility to pass resolutions without the need for the shareholders to be physically present.]

7 *A director may vote in respect of any contract, appointment or arrangement in which he is interested, and he shall be counted in the quorum present at the meeting.*
[This paragraph ignores conflicts of interest.]

8 *The directors may exercise the voting powers conferred by the shares of any other company held or owned by the company in such manner in all respects as they think fit and in particular they may exercise the voting powers in favour of any resolution appointing the directors or any of them as directors or officers of such other company or providing for the payment of remuneration or pensions to the directors or officers of such other company. Any director of the company may vote in favour of the exercise of such voting rights, notwithstanding that he may be or may be about to become a director or officer of such other company, and as such or in any other manner is or may be interested in the exercise of such voting rights in manner aforesaid.*

9 *Any director may from time to time appoint any person who is approved by the majority of the directors to be an alternate or substitute director. The appointee, while he holds office as an alternate director, shall be entitled to notice of meetings of the directors and to attend and vote thereat as a director and shall not*

be entitled to be remunerated otherwise than out of the remuneration of the director appointing him. Any appointment under this regulation shall be effected by notice in writing given by the appointer to the secretary. Any appointment so made may be revoked at any time by the appointer or by a majority of the other directors or by the company in general meeting.

Revocation by an appointer shall be effected by notice in writing given by the appointer to the secretary.

Note: Regulations 3, 4 and 5 of this Part are alternative to regulations 24, 51 and 54 respectively of Part I. Regulations 7 and 8 of this Part are alternative to regulations 84 and 86 of Part I.

Appendix 3: Table B

Table B in the Companies Act 1963 is the standard Memorandum of Association adopted by most companies. Draft your company's Memorandum based on the following, including any amendments you feel necessary (see section Memorandum of Association, page 11).

Table B

Form of Memorandum of Association of a Company Limited by Shares

1. The name of the company is "The Western Mining Company, Limited".

2. The objects for which the company is established are the mining of minerals of all kinds and the doing of such other things as are incidental or conducive to the attainment of the above object.
   [This is the "Objects" clause, which sets out the purposes for which the company has been set up.]

3. The liability of the members is limited.

4. The share capital of the company is £200,000, divided into 200,000 shares of £1 each.
   [This paragraph sets out the nominal share capital of the company and explains how it is divided.]

   We, the several persons whose names and addresses are subscribed, wish to be formed into a company in pursuance of this memorandum of association, and we agree to take the number of shares in the capital of the company set opposite our respective names.

Names, Addresses and Descriptions of Subscribers	*Number of Shares taken by each subscriber*
(Name of first subscriber) of (address) ..... in the County of ..... , (business occupation).	*One*
(Name of second subscriber) of (address) ..... in the County of ..... , (business occupation).	*One*
Total Shares taken	*Two*

Signed: (Subscribers' signatures)
Dated the ..... day of ..... , 20..
Witness to the above signatures: